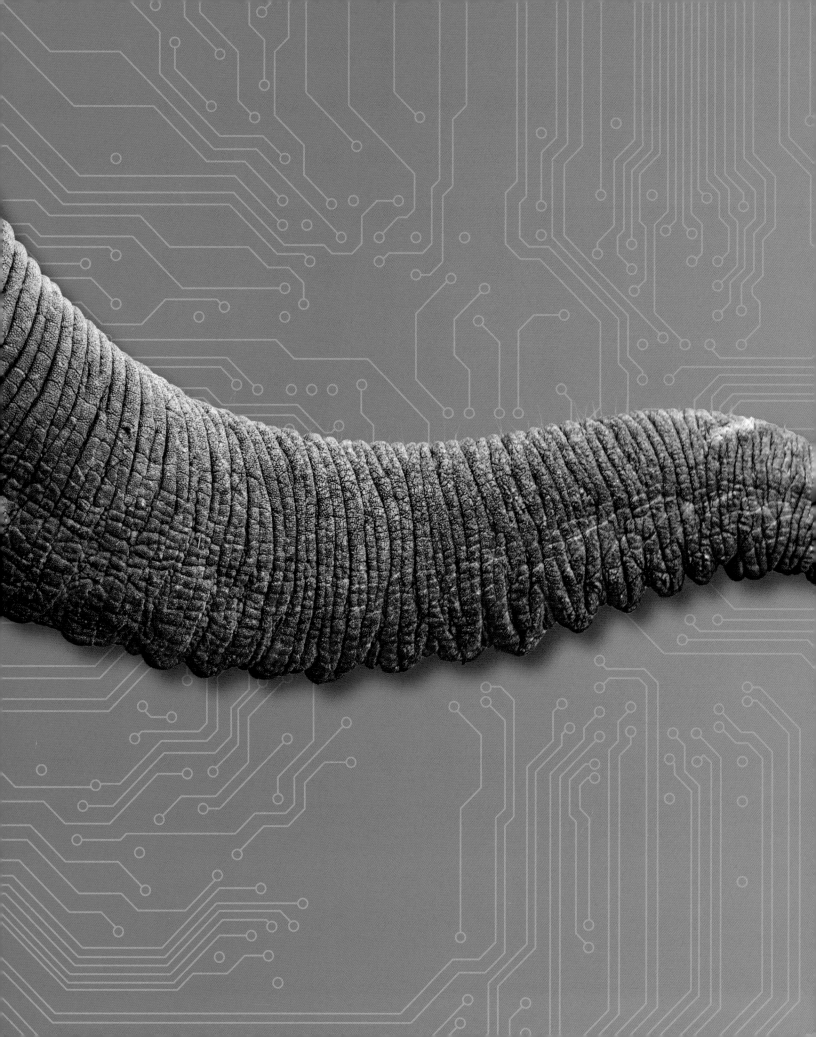

# BEASTLY BIONICS

## RAD ROBOTS, BRILLIANT BIOMIMICRY, AND INCREDIBLE INVENTIONS INSPIRED BY NATURE

JENNIFER SWANSON

NATIONAL GEOGRAPHIC
WASHINGTON, D.C.

# CONTENTS

# INTRODUCTION

▶ STICKY FEET TO CLIMB WALLS. ULTRAFLEXIBLE ROBOTIC ARMS. SUPERSENSITIVE HEARING. ARE THESE ABILITIES ONLY FOUND IN MOVIES? NO! THEY'RE TECHNOLOGIES MADE WITH BIONICS.

When you hear the word "bionic," you might think of robotic body parts. But bionics—a combination of the words "biology" and "electronics"—means so much more than making robotic limbs. It is engineering inspired by biology or nature.

Looking to nature is useful! For example, if you needed to build a robot that could move long distances across flat ground, you could study animals that can do that. Maybe kangaroos would work. They cover a lot of distance when they jump. To make a robot kangaroo, you'd need to understand how kangaroos move, how they crouch and then push off with their two hind legs to jump into the air. Then you'd have to figure out how to copy that movement with gears, motors, metals, and plastic. That can be a challenge. But in 2014, engineers actually succeeded in creating a bionic robot that hops like a kangaroo.

The borrowed movement of a real kangaroo is called biomimicry, or "biomimetics," a word that means "to imitate designs from biology." Biomimicry isn't limited to robots. Many different areas of study use bionics: architecture, transportation, energy, medicine, farming, and even communication. Because nature has already solved some challenges humans face, it's the perfect place to find ways to help.

Think of the possibilities! You could build a tsunami early-warning system based on the way dolphins communicate with one another. You could climb really fast and really high by mimicking the gecko, or quickly repair broken bones by copying the glue from the sandcastle worm. It's innovation in action! Sound intriguing? If so, get ready to meet some awesome bionic creations inspired by amazing animals!

▲ WITH ITS "STICKY FEET," THIS ROBOTIC GECKO CAN CLIMB ALMOST AS WELL AS THE ONE FOUND IN NATURE.

This book is chock-full of biomimetic inventions. We break down each with info in a few different categories:

AMAZING ANIMAL—The incredible, inspirational animal

DESIGN DILEMMA—The challenge engineers needed to solve

BUILDING BIONICS—All the amazing info of how the technology was created

HELPFUL ADDITIONS—Useful add-ons to the technology that the original animal doesn't have

GOING FURTHER—A supercool extra fact about the technology

DID YOU KNOW?—A fascinating fact about the awesome animal

## THREE TERMS USED THROUGHOUT THIS BOOK

BIONICS: the study of nature to engineer modern technology

BIOMIMICRY: to copy designs from nature. Term comes from "bio," as in "biology" (meaning "life"), and "mimesis," or "mimicking" (meaning "to copy")

BIOMIMETICS: the study of the structure and function of living things as models for new designs

# CHAPTER 1

# BEASTLY SOLUTIONS

▶ **THE DAMPNESS OF THE COOL DIRT** seeps through your clothes as you lie still on the ground. It is tough not to squirm, as you think about all the creepy-crawly ants and worms that must lie beneath the soil. But you stay still. You are, after all, hiding from your best friend because this is the day you are determined to win hide-and-seek.

Suddenly, four white, spindly legs appear over the rocky hill above you. Then four more legs and a chubby, hairless body follow. A spider! And a giant one, too. It must be two feet (0.6 m) or more across. It's headed right for you. What do you do? You can't run—if you do, you'll be found. Maybe it won't see you ...

No luck. The spider moves closer. Your body tenses. When it reaches your hand, you grab it. As you pick it up, you notice the tiny camera, focusing right on you.

Gotcha! Your friend wins again. Of course, it wasn't exactly fair using a robot spider to find you.

Designed to squeeze through small spaces, crawl through underground tunnels, and navigate over rocky terrain, this spider is not really made to play with. It is actually programmed for search and rescue operations. It can help find people trapped inside buildings after natural disasters, such as fires or earthquakes.

The spider is just one of the many different biomimetic inventions described in this chapter. Others include extrastrong helmets designed like the head of a hummingbird and body armor modeled after turtle shells. There's even a way to remove ice from planes by mimicking the skin of a poison dart frog. All of these biomimetic creations are designed to provide solutions to many complex problems.

Did You **KNOW?**

It's estimated that you are never more than 10 feet (3 m) away from a **SPIDER.**

## GOING **FURTHER**

**THE BEST PART** about the robot spider? It can be created using a **3D PRINTER.** Joints printed with soft plastics are connected by hinges. The hinges allow for movement to make the **SPIDER CRAWL.**

# LIFESAVING SPIDERS

## Amazing Animal
## SPIDER

**THIS EIGHT-LEGGED CREATURE** moves around easily and is small enough to fit into tiny places. With flexible joints in their legs, spiders can get just about anywhere. Spiders also have small hairs on their legs that help them cling to ceilings and walls.

## DESIGN DILEMMA

**AFTER A BUILDING COLLAPSES,** it is very important that rescuers get to anyone who might be trapped inside—fast. The problem is: How do search and rescue teams know where to look for survivors? Some buildings are huge! People or animals could be trapped anywhere inside. If the rescue team had something that could crawl through the debris to give them a good look inside, that would certainly help. Damaged buildings can also be dangerous places. Crumbling walls, smoke, and dust could injure rescuers, requiring them to be rescued themselves! A robot could help. Maybe it would even assist rescuers in finding a safe path through the building that wouldn't cause another cave-in. What kind of robot could help in this dangerous, high-stakes situation? Thanks to the spider, engineers had a solution.

▲ RESCUE TEAMS SEARCH THROUGH A COLLAPSED BUILDING FOR SURVIVORS.

## BUILDING BIONICS

**THE BIG CHALLENGE** for engineers when designing a robot for this task was to create one that was small, flexible, and could move around obstacles easily. The robot would also need to be able to move around on its own. In addition, it would need to run on a battery instead of being plugged into an outlet. The engineers thought a spider would be a great animal model.

It's not easy to build a robot spider with lots of moving parts. After all, a spider has eight legs, each of which can rotate, flex, and extend on its own. Each leg is made up of seven different segments connected by tiny joints. For a spider to move, it needs to pump a bloodlike fluid through its joints. This allows the spider to move different parts of each leg as it walks.

In addition to moving its joints, a spider keeps four legs on the ground at a time as it walks. Two legs pull forward while two others push from the back. The four that are not on the ground rotate and get ready to take the next step. The spider repeats this pattern over and over as it scuttles across the ground.

To make the robot spider walk, engineers needed to create thousands of lines of computer code, with directions telling the robot how to work its legs. This included building up pressure in its legs and instructing the artificial hinges to open and close like joints. This process made the legs extend like a real spider's. The robot spider is larger than a real spider because its valves, compressors, and control unit all must be contained inside its body. Even so, these leggy machines will be very useful at disaster sites.

### HELPFUL ADDITIONS
Robot spiders are equipped with a camera and sensors. These are designed to send back information, such as location and warnings about possible dangers.

# SPIDER MANIA

**S**PIDERWEBS ARE MADE FROM some of the strongest material on the planet. This material varies from spider to spider, but some webs are as strong as or even stronger than steel in the amount of force they can handle before they break. Webs are flexible, sticky, and above all, can be woven into many different patterns. There are so many different uses for biomimetic spiderwebs! Check out some clever ways these webs can help humans out of sticky situations.

▼ EACH STRAND OF SPIDERWEB SILK IS MADE OF THOUSANDS OF TINY THREADS COMBINED, WHICH MAKES THE SILK ONE OF THE STRONGEST MATERIALS IN NATURE.

## MATERIAL THAT DECOMPOSES WHEN WET

**WHAT DO YOU DO WITH OLD, WORN-OUT SNEAKERS?** Most people throw them away. But one shoe company has created running shoes that are mostly **BIODEGRADABLE.** To do this, the company used **ARTIFICIAL SPIDER SILK THAT DISINTEGRATES—** or falls apart. Of course, the shoes don't fall apart while they're on your feet. You have to put them in the sink and add water and a **SPECIAL ENZYME** to help break down the threads. After the shoes disintegrate, all that's left are the soles. You simply **WASH THE LIQUEFIED SHOES DOWN THE DRAIN,** but you'll have to toss the soles in the trash.

## MATERIALS THAT CAPTURE WATER IN SPACE

**SPIDERWEBS** in nature are able to hold many things: the spider, insects, and **EVEN WATER DROPLETS.** Students at the University of Calgary in Canada investigated ways to create a **WEB-LIKE STRUCTURE** that would not only hold water, but would also **ATTRACT WATER VAPOR FROM A PLANET'S ATMOSPHERE.** Have you ever seen a spiderweb covered with dew in the morning? The **SPIDERWEBS IN SPACE** would work in the same way. Water would be attracted to a dry web and leave the atmosphere, collecting on the strands as **TINY DROPLETS.** This would be critical for **ESTABLISHING A HOME** on planets with very little liquid, **SUCH AS MARS.**

## MATERIALS TO BUILD OBJECTS IN SPACE

NASA is studying the use of **SPIDERLIKE DROIDS** to build **GIANT SPACE OBJECTS,** such as satellites, radio antennae, and solar arrays, from parts sent up into space. The droids will combine materials, such as **CARBON FIBERS,** in much the same way as a **SPIDER SPINS A WEB.** The fibers will attach the parts to one another, building the machinery or other objects. This means there would be no need for expensive missions to transport objects to space after they are created on the ground—only the raw materials would need to be sent. Sounds like a very **OUT-OF-THIS-WORLD IDEA!**

# BIRDLIKE BULLET TRAINS

**A SMALL, BRIGHTLY COLORED BIRD** measuring no more than 6.7 to 7.5 inches (17 to 19 cm) long, the common kingfisher lives near bodies of water on all the continents except Antarctica. What is its best bionic feature? A very useful streamlined beak.

## DESIGN DILEMMA

**WHAT DO YOU DO WHEN** you create a train that moves so fast it creates a huge boom? Ask a team of engineers in Japan, led by Eiji Nakatsu. The bullet trains in Japan carry more than 420,000 passengers a weekday, whisking people more than 310 miles (500 km) in less than two and a half hours. That's more than twice as fast as a car drives on the highway!

The trains saved lots of time, but their big boom was a bummer. It turns out that the trains moved so fast through tunnels that a pocket of air would build up around the nose, or front, of the train. When a train burst out of a tunnel, this air pocket collapsed all at once, making the gigantic booming sound. The loud noise disturbed people and animals living nearby. The train engineers were stumped as to how to solve this problem—until they studied the narrow, needlelike beak of the kingfisher.

### HELPFUL ADDITIONS
Do you feel the speed of a bullet train as it zooms down the tracks? Nope. Bullet trains are pressurized inside, just like airplanes. You don't feel a thing.

## BUILDING BIONICS

**WITH ITS POINTED BEAK**, the king-fisher easily plunges into the water without creating much of a ripple—almost like a needle and thread poking through cloth. Engineers thought that the bird's pointed beak might be an ideal model for a train.

When Nakatsu and his team studied the nose of the bullet train, they discovered that a train with a flat nose created a big air pocket. A nose that was more streamlined, however, allowed air to flow around it. This reduced the friction, or the pushing back, of air against the train. The air pocket did not form.

The team tested different nose shapes against air pressure in a scale model tunnel, and the nose modeled after the kingfisher worked the best. Then they tried the new nose on a train.

It worked! Soon, all of the Shinkansen trains were sporting a needle nose. The booming was elimi-nated, and people and animals living near the tunnels were no longer bothered by excessive noise.

◄ THE SHINKANSEN BULLET TRAIN QUIETLY PULLS INTO THE TOKYO STATION.

## GOING **FURTHER**

THE LOUD BOOMING made by a BULLET TRAIN is not a SONIC BOOM. A true sonic boom is heard for many miles. It happens when an object, usually a military jet or spacecraft, TRAVELS FASTER THAN SOUND. The sound waves created by the aircraft pile up around it until multiple sound waves BURST FORTH IN A GIANT BOOM! The speed of sound is often thought to be at 768 MILES AN HOUR (1,236 km/h). Bullet trains travel at speeds close to 200 miles an hour (320 km/h), so they are not fast enough to break the SPEED OF SOUND.

### Did You KNOW?

KINGFISHERS don't live in nests. Instead, they burrow small holes in the dirt along riverbanks or in trees. They build these holes with their feet, not their long bills.

# ADAPTABLE SEA STAR

## Amazing Animal
## SEA STAR

**OFTEN CALLED STARFISH** even though they are not fish, sea stars usually have five arms, but some varieties have even more. Capable of living anywhere from the cold seafloor to warm tropical waters, sea stars' most notable feature is that they can adapt if they lose a limb.

## DESIGN DILEMMA

**ROBOTS BREAK.** After all, they have hundreds, even thousands, of tiny parts. It's a big problem if robots break when they are far from home, like deep underwater or in space. How do you fix a robot that needs to move around when you can't get to it? Years of hard work and a lot of money could be lost if researchers can't retrieve the broken bot. Never fear, said the researchers at Cornell University in New York State, U.S.A. They designed a walking robot that can adapt to losing a limb.

### HELPFUL ADDITIONS
If humans want to live on Mars one day, they may use this Starfish robot as a model for technology that can adapt to life on another planet.

▲ A STARFISH ROBOT CAN LEARN TO ADAPT TO LOSING A LEG, JUST LIKE A STARFISH, OR SEA STAR, IN NATURE MUST DO.

## BUILDING BIONICS

**SCIENTISTS HAVE DEVELOPED A** four-legged robot, called Starfish, that is programmed differently from many other robots. It is not given exact instructions. Instead, it can discover its own abilities.

The Starfish robot has a unique way of "thinking." Engineers created the robot so that it recognizes the location of its legs and then programmed it to move forward. But the robot is not told how to use its legs for walking. It must figure that out for itself.

How does it do that? The way any human baby would: by falling, getting back up, and trying again. Through this process, the Starfish—made from 3D-printed soft plastic—learns how to use its four legs equally to balance while walking. It can take a long time and many attempts to get it right, but eventually, the robot learns how to walk.

The Starfish walks by sending wireless signals to 15 different computers. The computers calculate the changes needed to make the robot move. This is repeated over and over until the robot "learns." Once the robot knows how to walk, researchers remove part of one of its legs, making the robot learn to walk all over again. Although the robot can't grow a new leg like the sea star, it can adapt to its situation.

◀ MOST SEA STAR SPECIES CAN GROW NEW ARMS OR EVEN MOST OF THEIR BODY, BUT REGROWING THESE PARTS CAN TAKE UP TO A YEAR OR MORE. THIS IS WHY A SEA STAR NEEDS TO LEARN HOW TO MOVE AROUND WHILE THE ARM OR BODY PART GROWS BACK.

# TURTLE BODY ARMOR

## Amazing Animal
### TURTLE

**AMONG THE OLDEST REPTILES** on the planet, turtles have been around for more than 220 million years and can be recognized by their hard outer shell. The shell not only acts as protection, but also as their home. How convenient!

## DESIGN DILEMMA

**SINCE THE DAWN OF CIVILIZATION,** humans have been searching for ways to arm and protect themselves. Roman soldiers wore heavy body armor for protection. They also carried shields that weighed as much as 22 pounds (10 kg). Although both of these objects came in handy during combat, they were extremely heavy to carry around. Soldiers needed to be able to move quickly in battle, and they couldn't do that with bulky, heavy armor.

Throughout history, armor began to get somewhat lighter, but the problem was that lighter materials didn't always protect the soldier as well. And it wasn't flexible, something that is also important for easy movement.

The other option for soldiers today is to use hard armor. The hard armor relies on a rigid core made from ceramic, a clay hardened by heat. The modern armor is still heavy to wear. It can slow down soldiers and make bending and walking difficult. So, how can modern soldiers stay safe and move around freely?

With the development of technologically advanced weapons, humans need new ways to keep safe. Engineers were called in to help solve this problem. They turned to bionics. Which animal would be the best to help with this problem? A turtle, of course.

◀ ANCIENT ARMOR WAS ROUNDED AND WORN ON TOP OF THE BODY FOR PROTECTION, JUST LIKE A TURTLE'S SHELL.

## BUILDING BIONICS

**A TURTLE IS** a great model for protection. Turtle shells are like a single reinforced piece of armor. The inside of the shell is made up of approximately 50 different bones that are part of the turtle's spine and rib cage. All of this structural support makes the shell very strong. When the shell is hit with something hard, the force spreads out along the spine and is absorbed. The turtle inside feels almost nothing because its shell doesn't even dent. Sounds like an excellent model for human body armor!

People can't attach shells to their spines, but they can wear armor over their bodies that works like a turtle's shell. Thanks to the work of engineers, today's military and law enforcement individuals use full-body armor with reinforced fabrics that act like the turtle spine and rib cage. The special fabrics help deflect bullets and keep sharp objects from penetrating the armor. Carbon fiber is used to make the armor, which is a flexible, lightweight, and very strong material. That makes the armor perfect for protecting humans. No shell or hard armor needed.

▲ SOLDIERS TRY ON TACTICAL VESTS OVER THEIR UNIFORMS.

**Did You KNOW?**

A **TURTLE'S SHELL** grows with the turtle as it grows in size. It is impossible for turtles to get bigger than their shells.

▼ CLOSE-UP VIEW OF FISH SCALES

## GOING **FURTHER**

**FISH HAVE ALSO** inspired body armor designs. Using small scales to break up hard armor makes the armor **EASIER FOR SOLDIERS TO BEND AND MOVE.** The scales can slide back and forth for **FLEXIBILITY.** This flexible armor is also much more comfortable to wear for long periods of time. And why not learn from fish? Like turtles, **THEY HAVE LIVED ON EARTH A LOT LONGER THAN HUMANS HAVE.**

# SHOCK-ABSORBING WOODPECKERS

## Amazing Animal
## WOODPECKER

**FOUND PRETTY MUCH EVERYWHERE** except Australia, Madagascar, New Zealand, and the North and South Poles, these pretty birds are known for the *rat-tat-tat* sound they make by pounding their tough beaks against trees.

### Did You KNOW?

**WOODPECKERS** are one of the few birds that can hop up a tree. That's because they have special zygodactyl toes. This means that two of their toes point forward and two point backward, giving them amazing gripping powers.

## DESIGN DILEMMA

**HOW DO YOU KEEP SOMETHING** from being damaged when it's involved in a collision? Finding that answer could make all kinds of things safer. Think of a football helmet. When one football player tackles another, they smack into each other. Hard. The impact can cause an athlete to get a concussion. The same problem exists with black boxes in airplanes. A black box records the plane's position in the air and communications between pilots and the airport. In a crash, the black box helps investigators get information about what happened. But if a black box falls thousands of feet and smashes into the ground, it could be useless. Developing a way to reduce damage to black boxes after a collision would be a huge accomplishment. Where do engineers start? By observing the woodpecker.

## GOING **FURTHER**

**WHAT IS G-FORCE?** The "g" stands for **GRAVITY.** A g-force is a unit that measures the force of gravity or **ACCELERATION ON AN OBJECT.** G-forces are used to describe how much force an object absorbs when it **IMPACTS, OR COLLIDES** with, something.

For a **WOODPECKER,** the quick back-and-forth movement of the **BIRD'S HEAD AGAINST A TREE WITH ITS BEAK** causes the bird to experience g-forces of more than 1,200 g's. In comparison, when **TWO FOOTBALL PLAYERS** crash into each other head-on, the force is between 80 and 100 g's. A **BLACK BOX** falling from a high altitude may experience 1,000 g's. The greater the g-force, **THE GREATER THE IMPACT.**

▼ FOOTBALL PLAYERS COLLIDE WHILE THEY TACKLE ONE ANOTHER.

# BUILDING BIONICS

**HEAR THAT HAMMERING COMING** from a nearby tree? That's the sound of natural engineering in action. A woodpecker can pound its pointy beak into the bark of a tree between 18 and 22 times a second. The bird is looking for the delicious grubs inside the tree, but engineers wanted to know how the woodpecker absorbs all that force without getting a massive headache.

They learned that the bird's head and beak are designed to absorb the force of hitting them against the tree. Unlike humans, who have very hard bones, a woodpecker's skull bones are spongy. That makes them flexible. A woodpecker has a special feature called a hyoid layer—a tongue bone and soft tissues that reduce vibration. The hyoid support system works kind of like a layer of rubber, spreading out the force of the *rat-a-tat* impact instead of focusing it all in one place.

To solve the problem of protecting an airplane's black box, engineers created a steel case. This case is made of material similar to that of a woodpecker's strong beak. To mimic the hyoid bone, they added rubber casing along the inside of the steel case, which cut down on vibration. Another thin layer of metal was added to act like the bird's protective skull. The engineers then placed closely packed glass beads inside the "skull" layer for that soft, spongy effect. Finally, they packed the black box in the middle.

Next, they tested the forces by blasting the box with a huge air gun. The result? The black box survived up to 60,000 g's of force. That's well over what it might experience from tumbling out of the sky and crashing to the ground. Success!

▲ DAMAGED AIRPLANE BLACK BOX AFTER A CRASH

# MANTA RAY SEARCH AND RESCUE

## Amazing Animal
## MANTA RAY

**A SILENT, MAJESTIC CREATURE OF THE DEEP,** this animal has wings that stretch more than 23 feet (7 m) across and look like smooth, gray capes. Its wings also make it a powerful swimmer.

## DESIGN DILEMMA

**OLYMPIC SWIMMERS MAY BE AWESOME,** but they are slowpokes compared to most animals that live in the water. Human bodies are not streamlined to glide through water like dolphins or fish. Plus, humans can only hold their breath underwater for about a minute at a time. We tend to turn to boats and scuba gear to move faster, especially in search and rescue missions at sea. But the problem with search and rescue boats is that they require regular refueling, limiting how far they can travel. Rescue missions can also be dangerous for scuba divers if they don't know where to look or what obstacles are in the way.

What if humans took inspiration from the manta ray? If humans could figure out how to create robots that would swim like these aquatic superheroes, rescuers could save more lives.

▼ THE MANTADROID SWIMS ABOUT 2.3 FEET (0.7 M) A SECOND AND CAN KEEP SWIMMING FOR UP TO 10 HOURS.

## BUILDING BIONICS

**FOR MORE THAN 30 YEARS,** scientists have been studying the unique way manta rays glide through water. Rays swim at about nine miles an hour (15 km/h)—nearly twice the speed of an Olympic swimmer—and can sprint up to 22 miles an hour (35 km/h) for short periods of time. Creating robotic wings that move up and down as smoothly as a manta ray's wings is complicated. Another issue is the material. How do you create something that is waterproof, but also extremely flexible so that water just flows right over it?

Dr. Chew Chee-Meng of the National University of Singapore finally put everything together. He and his team designed a robotic version of a manta ray, which he called the MantaDroid. At about 14 inches (35 cm) long, with a 25-inch (63-cm) wingspan, the MantaDroid is much smaller than an actual manta ray. Yet, it is able to swim in a similar manner.

Like an actual manta ray, the MantaDroid has two wings and two fins. Chew began by using a single electric motor for each wing. This reduced the overall weight of the robot. Then his team constructed the fins out of PVC: a smooth, waterproof plastic that allows water to slide easily across the robot. The PVC material is very flexible and allows the robot to change direction quickly and easily. Every time it flaps its wings, it travels one body length. Perhaps in the future, MantaDroids will be used to search for lost divers or even hunt for sunken treasure.

## Did You KNOW?

**MANTA RAYS** must swim constantly to stay alive. They travel about 43 miles (69 km) underwater every day.

## GOING **FURTHER**

**CHEW AND HIS TEAM** are working on a **MANTA RAY ROBOT** twice the size of MantaDroid. He hopes to be able to use it to **GATHER DATA** from the ocean about its **BIODIVERSITY**, which includes the **NUMBERS AND SPECIES OF ANIMALS**, as well as **OCEAN TEMPERATURES** and their effects on **CLIMATE CHANGE**.

# FASCINATING FROG SKIN

## Amazing Animal
## POISON DART FROG

**THIS VIBRANTLY** colored amphibian is one of the most toxic animals on the planet. It protects itself with a thin film of poison on its outer skin. Predators beware!

## DESIGN DILEMMA

**HAVE YOU EVER SEEN A PLANE BEING DE-ICED?** It happens in winter when ice and snow build up on the wings and body of a plane. These must be removed before the plane takes off for a variety of reasons. First of all, snow and ice can change a plane's shape and make it heavier. Ice also keeps the wings from moving properly. An airplane's wings are curved from front to back and have flaps, or moving sections, that can be extended to make the wings wider. If any of these parts are covered in snow and ice, they won't move quickly and easily when the pilot needs them to.

The ice also increases the wing's size, which causes air to flow over it differently. Too much ice on a wing can make the plane lose altitude, or go lower in the air than planned. That is dangerous for the plane. For that reason, any ice and snow that builds up on the plane needs to be removed as quickly as possible, and even during flight, it can't accumulate. To fix the problem of planes icing up, engineers wanted to create a liquid mixture that would not only remove snow and ice, but would also keep both from collecting on the plane during flight. This is where the poison dart frog's secret power comes in.

▲ CHEMICALS ARE SPRAYED ONTO A PASSENGER PLANE TO DE-ICE IT.

## BUILDING BIONICS

**THE POISON DART FROG** is the perfect animal to mimic for this solution. It has a double layer of skin. The inner layer of its skin holds the poison. The outer layer is safe to touch—until the frog gets scared. Then the frog releases the toxin, which comes up through the skin and coats the outer layer with poison.

Dr. Konrad Rykaczewski and his team at Arizona State University, U.S.A., thought mimicking the poison dart frog's double-layer skin would be just the thing to help de-ice planes. Their first step was to create a two-layered system of delivering antifreeze to a plane. Antifreeze is a solution made up of water and a chemical called glycol that prevents freezing.

Currently, antifreeze is sprayed onto airplanes before they take off. This removes all the snow and ice. Then, a layer of anti-icing fluid is applied to prevent the ice from re-forming on the plane during flight. After takeoff, hot air from the engines flow over the wings and tail, keeping it ice free. This process doesn't always work well in mid-flight, however. So, the team of scientists decided to use the dart frog to come up with a better solution.

Rykaczewski and his team decided to spray two paper-thin layers of liquid onto the airplane. Just like the frog's two layers. The bottom layer is antifreeze to remove the ice. The top layer is designed to repel water, like snow and ice, by making the water bead up on the outside of the plane.

If the top layer starts to freeze up, the ice particles fall through the top layer and make contact with the bottom layer of antifreeze. This causes the ice to melt, and the plane de-ices itself in midair. This is the opposite of what happens in the frog. The dart frog secretes the poison up through its skin. On the plane, the ice drops down through the layers and dissolves. Either way, it's a pretty cool concept for both the plane and the frog!

▶ RYKACZEWSKI APPLIES FLUID TO A PIECE OF BIONIC FROG SKIN TO TEST ITS HYDROPHOBIC COATING.

## GOING **FURTHER**

**FAILURE IS NOT SOMETHING THAT PREVENTS ENGINEERS FROM MOVING FORWARD**—sometimes it is the **ANSWER TO THE QUESTION.** Engineers often need to do many different trials to find the **RIGHT SOLUTION** to a problem, as they did when creating this material. Think about that the next time you fail at something. **INSTEAD OF GIVING UP,** think like an engineer. **USE FAILURE TO YOUR ADVANTAGE!**

**Did You KNOW?**

BATS are the only mammal that can fly.

## GOING FURTHER

ALTHOUGH THE BAT BOT only works for SHORT FLIGHTS, it may perhaps TAKE TO THE SKIES one day and SOAR WITH REAL BATS in the wild. Also, this BAT BOT IS SOFT, so if one flies into your head, IT WON'T HURT ... MUCH.

# BAT DELIVERY

## Amazing Animal
### BAT

**THESE SMALL,** winged mammals fly almost noiselessly through the sky. They have built-in sonar to "see" at night.

◀ BAT BOT'S BODY IS MADE OF ELECTRONICS AND WIRES THAT HELP ITS WINGS MOVE ALMOST EFFORTLESSLY.

## DESIGN DILEMMA

**IMAGINE THIS:** You need to distribute lots of supplies in a hospital emergency room, and you need to do it fast. Most of the doctors and nurses are already busy taking care of patients. It's up to you, the student volunteer, to help. How are you going to do it? It will take a long time if you have to keep going back and forth to the supply closet, restocking each room as needed. What you really need is a helper. One that could carry supplies quickly and easily, maybe by flying over the heads of the busy medical staff so that it doesn't bother them in their duties. But where can you find such a helper?

Ask a bat. No, not a real one, but a robot bat called Bat Bot. This bat could deliver small items throughout a hospital or construction site, or even in your own home. Engineers are working on technology that could do just this.

## BUILDING BIONICS

**THE BIGGEST CHALLENGE** in creating a robotic bat is the wings. Each bat wing has 20 to 25 different joints, making it extremely flexible. By moving only a few bones at a time, bats can shape their wings to dive, soar, and even glide along wind currents with ease.

Copying the 40 to 50 bones in both wings combined would be a tough feat. Ultimately, the engineers settled for copying just the nine most important ones.

For the robot bat to fly, everything on it must be very lightweight. That is why it weighs less than 3.5 ounces (100 g)—or about as much as the weight of two golf balls.

Besides needing tiny motors, the robot bat also needed a light and flexible material for the wings. So, the engineers decided on a superthin silicone layer that's only about half the thickness of a human hair. This material allows the Bat Bot to stretch its wings and catch the air, sort of like a sail on a sailboat.

Did it work? Yes! The Bat Bot can fly straight or roll on its side to turn. Its normal speed is about 12 miles an hour (19 km/h), but when it dives, it can go as fast as 30 miles an hour (48 km/h). Future additions to the Bat Bot may include adding a way to hold things so that it can transport materials from place to place.

# CAT EYES LEAD TO A
# BRIGHT IDEA

**B**ACK IN 1933, a cat possibly saved a man's life—and gave him a bright idea. One night, Percy Shaw was driving home along a dark road, winding around the curves with not a single streetlight to guide him. Suddenly, he saw a flash of light in his rearview mirror. Curious, Shaw stopped and got out of the car for a closer look. The light turned out to be the glowing eyes of a cat. It was an unusual sight, but also a very lucky one for Shaw. As he returned to his car, Shaw discovered that he had been driving down the wrong side of the road. If he had continued, he could have missed his turn and driven off a cliff!

Shaw was quite a mechanical whiz, and seeing the cat's glow-in-the-dark eyes got him thinking. If he could make lights that reflected brightly in the dark, just like a cat's eyes, that invention would improve safety.

He set to work, creating a reflector, a piece of glass that would reflect the glow of headlights back at the driver. He figured that if the reflectors were small and placed along the edges and middle of a road, then drivers would be able to stay in their lane more easily. Called Catseye reflectors, they had a cast-iron base that contained a piece of rubber to hold each glass reflector in place.

Catseye reflectors are still used on many roads today, but the original idea is also seen in reflective road studs—white marks along the center or sides of a lane. Today's roads are safer, thanks to one lucky inventor and a bright-eyed cat.

◀ THESE REFLECTORS ON A ROAD LOOK JUST LIKE A PAIR OF CAT EYES.

**A CAT'S EYES DON'T ACTUALLY GLOW IN THE DARK.** They reflect the light already available. Eye shine is caused by the tapetum lucidum, a part of the eye that is its own reflective layer. When light shines into a cat's eyes, the tapetum lucidum reflects the light like a mirror, allowing the cat's eyes to capture more light than an eye without this special part. This gives the cat the appearance of glowing eyes. Eye shine allows animals to see their prey when hunting at night.

Did You **KNOW?**

Many animals have **REFLECTIVE EYES,** including spiders, alligators, and bullfrogs.

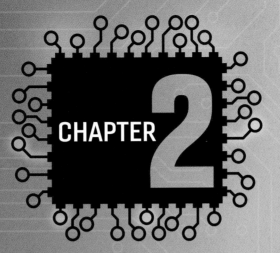

# CHAPTER 2

# BEASTLY HELPERS

▶**YOU'VE DECIDED TO MAKE SOME** cookies after school. You begin to gather the ingredients: flour, sugar, baking soda, chocolate chips, and so on. The thing is, the cabinets in your kitchen are really high. To reach everything, you have to drag a chair around the kitchen. You climb up, stretch to reach the ingredient you need, then climb back down. About now, you might be wishing that you were an elephant and could reach your trunk out and up to grab what you need. Then you could stay on the ground and still reach the items in those top cabinets. As it turns out, engineers have been developing a long, stretchy robotic elephant arm, designed just like an elephant's trunk, to help humans. And while you could possibly use a robotic trunk to help you with your baking dilemma, it could also do so much more. The trunk could help surgeons during operations. It could also be a huge help to people with disabilities.

Whatever their purpose, the bionic-inspired creations described in this chapter assist humans with everyday situations. In these pages, you'll learn about inventions that help protect food supplies, provide color-changing camouflage, warn people about giant ocean waves called tsunamis, and investigate ways to keep buildings cool more efficiently.

# ELEPHANT TRUNK TECHNOLOGY

## Amazing Animal
## ELEPHANT

**A LARGE LAND-BASED ANIMAL** found in the wild in Asia and Africa, the elephant has a big, bulky body and a long, flexible trunk. The trunk is strong enough to rip a small tree out of the ground, yet gentle enough to hug a newborn elephant calf. The trunk is an incredibly helpful tool.

## DESIGN DILEMMA

**MANY PEOPLE NEED HELP** lifting and moving objects safely. Factory and warehouse workers have to move large machinery or lift heavy boxes up to high shelves, and some people may not be able to grip, lift, or grab objects themselves. In these situations, and many others, a robotic arm could make tasks like these easier and much safer. Elephants have just the thing to help solve this problem.

### HELPFUL ADDITIONS
In the future, the robotic "elephant" arm will have a 3D camera that will allow it to avoid obstacles, including people.

◀ THE BIONIC HANDLING ASSISTANT IS ABLE TO LIFT AND MOVE OBJECTS OF DIFFERENT SIZES AND WEIGHTS.

## BUILDING BIONICS

**TO HELP WITH THE HEAVY LIFTING,** engineers looked to the amazing ways an elephant uses its trunk—one of the most flexible body parts in the animal kingdom. The trunk's primary job is to act as a nose for the elephant, but it does so much more.

An elephant uses its trunk to grab tasty leaves from trees and to suck up water and shoot it into its mouth or spray its body when taking a bath. And the trunk can move in pretty much every direction. It can throw heavy objects and lift tiny things quite delicately.

So, what would a trunk for humans look like? Engineers created an armlike tool called a Bionic Handling Assistant. Each arm is made up of as many as 48 plastic sections, depending on how the arm will be used. The sections make the arm more flexible. Each section contains a spring that's controlled by an actuator—a valve that opens and closes. This makes the section move, much like a muscle.

The extra flexibility of the arm makes it simple to use in enclosed spaces, such as your house or an operating room. The arm is lightweight, so moving it does not require too much energy. And a four-fingered claw on the end of the arm allows it to pick up small objects without crushing them. Now that's a handy invention!

## GOING **FURTHER**

There are different ways to make **ROBOTIC ARMS** move. The **BIONIC HANDLING ASSISTANT** relies on **ACTUATORS THAT WORK LIKE SPRINGS,** but engineers at the same company created another robotic arm with a **DIFFERENT DESIGN.** The other arm has sections made up of **HOLLOW CHAMBERS.** When air is **FORCED THROUGH** these chambers, it creates **PRESSURE,** causing the arm to **MOVE IN A PARTICULAR DIRECTION.**

# CEPHALOPOD CAMOUFLAGE

## *Amazing Animal*
## SQUID, OCTOPUS, AND CUTTLEFISH

**THESE MULTIARMED AQUATIC ANIMALS** are shape-shifters. Belonging to a group of animals called cephalopods, these sea creatures can change their size, form, and even their colors!

### DESIGN DILEMMA

**MILITARIES** around the world need their soldiers to blend in with their surroundings. Sometimes they don't know what colors they'll need to wear until they get to their mission site. Meanwhile, rescuers need to stand out so that the people in trouble, as well as the rest of the rescue team, can see them.

The problem is that sometimes soldiers need to quickly change the colors they wear when moving between environments—from a forest to a desert, for example. In the case of rescuers, what if they don't have red jackets to stand out in an avalanche?

Wouldn't it be great if they had one set of clothes that could change to the colors they needed automatically? It's time to turn to cephalopods like the octopus, cuttlefish, and squid. These animals know how to use camouflage!

### BUILDING BIONICS

**CEPHALOPODS CHANGE COLOR** by using sacs, called chromatophores, on their skin. They inflate the sacs by squeezing their muscles, which causes the sacs to expand. As the sacs expand, they change color, depending upon which colors the cephalopod needs. A cephalopod will match the color of sand or rocks, but if it moves over a coral reef, it will change to brighter colors to match the reef.

To mimic these masters of disguise, one set of engineers created a wearable material made of multiple layers. The top layer contains the pigments, the middle layer makes the color change, and the bottom layer senses which colors are needed for the change. Once the bottom layer decides on the color, it communicates that information to the middle layer through a sensor. The middle layer then changes its temperature to tell the top layer what colors to show. The result is a change in color to the skin. Because so many sensors are involved, the robotic material takes longer to change than a cephalopod takes to adapt, but it still works.

Another set of researchers tried a different approach to change textures. This skin is made of a rubberlike material called silicone, and it has a layer of mesh underneath. The mesh contains pockets that inflate like little balloons, changing the skin's texture.

◀ TINY COLOR-CHANGING SACS, OR CHROMATOPHORES, ON A SQUID

## GOING **FURTHER**

**SURE, COLOR-CHANGING CLOTHES** would be great for **SEARCH AND RESCUE MISSIONS,** but what about **HIGH FASHION** in the future? Need a pair of pants to go with your new shirt, but don't have time to shop? **CHANGE THE COLOR OF THE PANTS IN YOUR CLOSET.** Or perhaps you want to change the look of your bedroom? Use **COLOR-CHANGING WALLPAPER. YOU COULD TRY A NEW SHADE EVERY DAY!**

# BOA CONSTRICTOR GRIPPERS

## Amazing Animal
## BOA CONSTRICTOR

**A LONG, THICK-BODIED SNAKE** that can grow to be 13 feet (4 m) long, a boa constrictor grabs its prey and wraps it tightly to hold on to it. This reptile is not venomous; instead, it has a powerful, squeezing grip.

## DESIGN DILEMMA

**SCIENTISTS USE UNDERWATER ROBOTS,** called remotely operated vehicles (ROVs), to explore the deepest parts of the ocean, where humans can't swim. Samples of living organisms from these remote areas offer scientists clues to how our planet was formed and to its health today. ROVs also allow scientists to study how marine life has adapted to these extreme environments, where it is bitterly cold and almost completely dark. But an ROV's mechanical arm can be a bit clumsy for collecting fragile samples of marine life like coral and shells.

How do you get a sample of something so fragile without destroying it? The arms on the ROV are more like claws and usually only open and close. They would easily crush a piece of coral. What can scientists do? They can take a hint from the boa constrictor.

Engineers mimicked the boa constrictor to design a gripper for an ROV that can reach into tight spaces and gently cradle tiny samples of marine life.

### HELPFUL ADDITIONS

The robotic underwater grippers come with different attachments. Besides the boa-inspired gripper, there is also a bellows-type gripper. This works by pushing fluid through the tubes to make them open and close.

### Did You KNOW?

The thicker the **BOA CONSTRICTOR** is, the stronger the squeezing grip it applies to its prey.

**A BOA CONSTRICTOR** captures prey by wrapping its coils around it and squeezing. It doesn't squeeze all at once. It gently but firmly wraps its body tighter and tighter, cradling its prey. Engineers wanted to mimic the snake's gentle squeezing motion for their grippers.

To make this soft underwater gripper, engineers used a specific type of robotics called soft robotics. This means that the robot or machine is built with materials that can be moved and shaped. The engineers used 3D printers to create a rein-forced plastic tube, which they filled with memory foam (the soft, thick foam used in some sneakers). They then inserted tiny motors inside the memory foam. This combination of materials and motors resulted in a gentle squeezing motion by the tubes. The next step was to make adjustments so that the squeezing is constant and of equal strength on all sides. The result? The gripper can grab a sample, gently hold it, and bring it to the surface undamaged for study.

## GOING **FURTHER**

**HUMANS SHOULD NOT TOUCH OR PICK UP CORAL** because it could **DAMAGE OR KILL IT.** The coral can also live where it's **TOO DEEP FOR HUMANS** to get up close, which is why scientists rely on **ROVs.** But wouldn't it be cool to **FEEL THE CORAL WITHOUT HURTING IT?** Someday, perhaps these **GRIPPERS** will not only pick up pieces of coral, but will also have **TINY SENSORS** that allow the person controlling the grippers to **SENSE THE TEXTURE** of the coral, too.

▲ SOFT GRIPPER "FINGERS" ALLOW THIS ROBOT TO GENTLY PICK UP OBJECTS.

# BRILLIANT BEES!

**D**ID YOU KNOW THAT BEES have inspired new techniques for pollinating plants, methods for mass computing, ways to take better pictures, and even important advances in studying the ocean? You could say they are bee-ing awesomely helpful to humans!

## BEE ROBOTS CAN STUDY THE OCEAN

Designed with **WINGS THAT FLAP AND ROTATE,** tiny **BEE ROBOTS** will gather information about the **HEALTH OF THE OCEAN** and marine life for scientists. **UNDERWATER, THE WINGS** paddle and allow the **BEE TO SWIM.** The robo-bee also has a **TINY CHEMISTRY LAB** inside it that converts water into hydrogen and oxygen gas. When a very small flame ignites the gas inside the bee, *BLAM!* The bee **SHOOTS OUT OF THE WATER,** ready for another task.

## BEES HELP YOU TAKE BETTER PHOTOS

**EVEN IN DIM LIGHT,** bees can tell that a flower is bright yellow. **CAMERAS, HOWEVER, CANNOT.** Have you ever taken a picture when the lighting is off? **MAYBE THINGS LOOK GRAY OR FADED?** That's because **CAMERAS CANNOT "SEE" COLORS** in dim light. Bees, however, **CAN SEE THE EXACT COLOR** of an object. They have **THREE UPWARD-FACING EYES** that measure the light from the sky and make adjustments. These adjustments allow them to **SEE THE ACTUAL COLOR** of something **IN VIVID TONES.** By using this same **COLOR-PROCESSING INFORMATION,** scientists are working to create **COMPUTER PROGRAMS** that will do the same for a camera.

## BEES KEEP THE INTERNET BUZZING

The **MAIN CHALLENGE** with **MAINTAINING THE INTERNET** is the **MASSIVE AMOUNT OF INFORMATION** that moves at **VERY FAST SPEEDS.** It is difficult to design a program that can **HANDLE ALL OF THE DIFFERENT REQUESTS** from users and **POINT THEM TO THE RESPONSES THEY NEED** in a **FAST AND EFFICIENT MANNER.**

**ENTER THE BEE.** Bees have an **ORGANIZED SYSTEM** in which they **WORK IN TEAMS** to hunt for flower nectar. The team spreads out and visits flowers **OVER A LARGE AREA** and then heads back to the hive. **THEY FOLLOW A PATTERN BASED ON TIME, DAY, AND WEATHER.** Bees also use a special **"WAGGLE" DANCE** to teach other bees how to **TARGET THE BEST PATCHES OF FLOWERS.**

By using a similar pattern and **CODING IT INTO THE INTERNET,** engineers have created ways for **COMPUTER SERVERS** to **RUN APPLICATIONS MORE EFFICIENTLY.** This helps people **SAVE TIME AND MONEY** when **USING TECHNOLOGY.**

# BEE BIONICS

**T**HE FRUITS, VEGETABLES, AND GRAINS THAT YOU FIND in grocery stores were at one time crops growing in fields. Pretty much every crop you can think of, from potatoes to brussels sprouts, requires pollination to grow. During pollination, pollen is transferred from one flower to another. One of the major pollinators is the bumblebee. Cold winters, an infestation of mites, diseases, and pesticides affect bee populations; this declining population then affects agriculture. Good thing scientists are working on a plan to help with this problem!

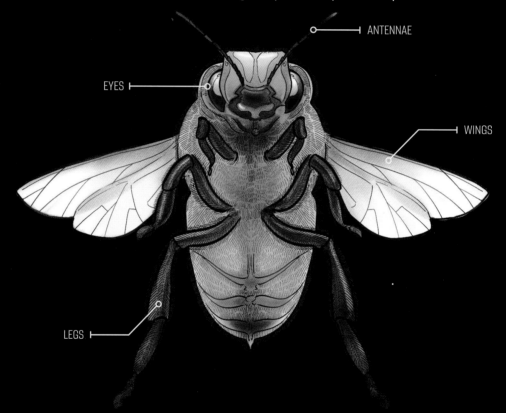

ANTENNAE

EYES

WINGS

LEGS

## BUMBLEBEE

**ANTENNAE:** These help bees smell pollen and other bees nearby.
**EYES:** A bee's eyes help it see far into the distance and give it a 3D view in flight.
**LEGS:** Bees use their back legs to collect pollen.
**WINGS:** Two pairs of wings help bees fly. Bumblebees quickly flap and rotate their wings at the same time to stay in the air.

**THE ROBOBEE IS ABOUT THE SIZE OF A QUARTER** and has very thin wings. The wings flap 120 times a second, allowing it to fly, hover, and steer itself into small spaces. The robotic wings are controlled independently and can be rotated, or moved in different directions, to keep the RoboBee upright in the air. Although it is slightly larger than a normal bee, the RoboBee is almost as maneuverable.

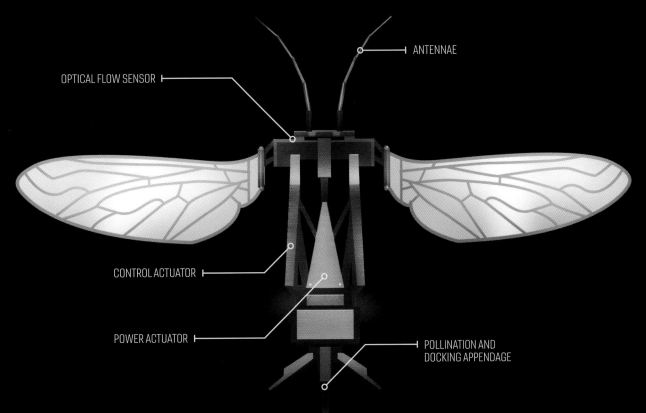

ANTENNAE

OPTICAL FLOW SENSOR

CONTROL ACTUATOR

POWER ACTUATOR

POLLINATION AND DOCKING APPENDAGE

## ROBOBEE

**ANTENNAE:** The RoboBee's antennae can sense changes in its environment, just like a real bee's.
**OPTICAL FLOW SENSOR:** This is an electronic sensor that allows the RoboBee to "see" objects moving at different distances away from it.
**CONTROL ACTUATORS:** These steer the wings in the right direction and control how they move.
**POWER ACTUATOR:** This powers the main flapping movement of the wings.
**POLLINATION AND DOCKING APPENDAGE:** Some RoboBee models will have special parts for landing and for transporting pollen.

### Did You KNOW?

**FISH** farming is called aquaculture, and it is one of the fastest-growing areas of food production.

# FISH FAKE-OUT

Amazing Animal
FISH

**FOUND IN BOTH** salt water and freshwater, these aquatic animals often swim in groups called schools. More than 30,000 different species live on our planet, and some species are caught in the wild or raised in enclosures for food.

## DESIGN DILEMMA

**FISH ARE AN EXCELLENT** source of protein, and a lot of people eat them. The average American eats 16 pounds (7 kg) of fish a year. Where does all this fish come from? Some comes from the wild, while some comes from fish farms. Yup, just like there are farms for raising cattle, there are also farms for raising fish—but they are underwater, of course!

Fish farms create an interesting problem. So many fish in one place sometimes create an unhealthy environment for the fish. For example, how can we be sure that the water is kept safe and clean so the fish don't pass diseases along to other ocean animals or humans?

To ensure the fish in a fish farm are healthy, farmworkers take water readings at many different places and depths. They use probes—instruments that are kind of like a thermometer—to test the water. The probes are attached to small robotic boats that move around an area to gather this information. Unfortunately, fish are afraid of these strange objects and they become stressed. If fish get too stressed, they can get very sick. This is not a good thing for a fish farm. What can researchers do? Perhaps make a fake fish robot to blend in with the school. Seriously. That is what they did.

▲ FISH FARMS FLOAT (IN THE ROUND CONTAINERS) OFF THE SHORES OF MARSEILLE, FRANCE.

## BUILDING BIONICS

**BUILDING A FISH ROBOT** involves a few steps. The robot must be able to mimic the smooth back-and-forth motion of a fish's tail. The robot also needs to be able to swim at different speeds, and dart up and down to copy a fish's movement. That's a pretty big requirement for technology that can be no bigger than about the size of two candy bars lined up end to end. The most important parts of this robot fish, however, are its sensors. Scientists need to be able to gather information about water temperature and pH level (a measure of how acidic or basic water is). The pH is a very reliable indicator of how healthy the water is. If the pH is too high or too low, the fish will die.

First, scientists made a robotic fish skeleton out of metal pieces. Within the skeleton, they placed tiny motors to mimic the side-to-side movement of a fish tail. This allows the fish robot to move through the water. Then they covered the whole skeleton with a polycarbonate, or a plastic, skin to make it look like a real fish. Finally, pH sensors were attached to the tail. The sensors gather information as the robot swims, and then send it wirelessly to a computer. When the robotic fish is placed in the fish farm, the real fish just ignore it. No stress here. Because the robotic fish work so well on fish farms, they have also been used to measure pH and temperature in the open ocean.

▶ THE BIONIC FISH'S SHAPE HELPS FOOL LIVE FISH.

# CLIMBING ROBOTIC INCHWORMS

## Amazing Animal
## INCHWORM

**THESE TINY ANIMALS** are actually larvae just waiting to turn into moths. They have feet on the front and back of their bodies and move by inching forward little by little.

## DESIGN DILEMMA

**CLIMBING TREES IS** not exactly an easy task for humans. Pulling yourself up a huge tree trunk without any low-hanging branches can require a rope, shoes with spikes, and a lot of effort. If the tree is really giant, you may need a crane that lifts you up while you stand in its basket. But why waste the effort if a robot can climb the tree for you? Researchers wanted to find a way to reach the treetops so that they could monitor a forest environment from above. The problem is getting there. It's hard for them to climb a tree while lugging all their equipment with them. Plus, some trees are so high that cranes cannot reach the top. Yet, the top of the forest canopy is the best place for scientists to gather this type of information. So they took inspiration from a champion crawler: the inchworm!

## BUILDING BIONICS

**INCHWORMS DON'T** move like many other animals. They don't have bones. Instead, they use their muscles to propel themselves along the ground. Each half of their body, or section, has two sets of muscles that allow the worm to grip the earth and pull itself forward. Circular muscles loop around each section, and long, straight muscles run the length of the body. An inchworm starts to move by stretching out its front feet and becoming longer. Then its midsection muscles contract, bringing the worm's back end forward. The inchworm then repeats this process. So, it appears as if it is "inching" along.

Researchers decided this action might work best to climb trees, so they built a robot that could move in a similar way. They created a body of flexible wire mesh. (Think of something like chicken wire with tiny holes between the wires.) Then they placed a motor and actuator—an automated part that allows the robot to move—on the inside. The robot is much bigger than an actual inchworm and doesn't look much like one either, but it does move like a worm. The creepy crawly can "inch" its way up a tree and gather climate information from the sensors in its body. Then the robot sends the data wirelessly back to the scientists on the ground.

▶ TREEBOT MOVES A LOT LIKE A REAL INCHWORM CLIMBING A TREE.

## Did You KNOW?

When sensing a predator, an **INCHWORM** becomes still and stands on its back legs to look like a twig.

**ROBOTS** that can **INCH FORWARD** could also be used to **CLIMB WALLS** or to **CLEAN YOUR WINDOWS** in the future. The possibilities are **ENDLESS.**

# ECO-FRIENDLY TERMITE-STYLE BUILDINGS

## Amazing Animal TERMITES

**THESE TINY INSECTS** live in colonies and create giant mounds with built-in temperature control. Their mounds' designs keep them cool.

## DESIGN DILEMMA

**IF YOU LIVE IN A PLACE** where the temperature gets warm enough to make you feel really hot, you will want a way to cool down. But what if you don't have access to air-conditioning? Or maybe the power sources are very expensive. It could be that you just want to find a way to be cool without affecting the environment much. How are you going to do that? Get used to being hot all the time? Hopefully not.

Constructing a building that can keep you cool naturally is not easy. It is also not cheap. Air-conditioning requires energy, and that has to come from somewhere. What if you could figure out a way to build a house that was easy to keep cool, energy efficient, and inexpensive?

To find that answer, engineers have been studying a little creature that is very good at building its own homes: the termite. Termites build massive tunnels that use the air in the atmosphere to keep cool. Wouldn't it be nice if humans could do that, too? As it turns out, they can.

## GOING FURTHER

Eventually, **ENGINEERS** hope to use **3D PRINTERS** to make **SPECIAL BUILDINGS** for people to live or sleep in— almost exactly **LIKE A TERMITE MOUND.**

▶ TERMITE MOUNDS CAN REACH UP TO 42 FEET (13 M) HIGH.

## Did You KNOW?

**TERMITES** never sleep (though some can go into a "frozen" state called diapause). They spend all day, every day, building and repairing their nests.

**A TERMITE MOUND LOOKS** like a really tall tube, or perhaps several tubes, or pipes. You could consider it an insect skyscraper compared to its tiny inhabitants. Of course, this skyscraper is made of soil, termite saliva (spit), and dung (poop). Don't worry, engineers aren't mimicking the termites' building materials to design a place for humans—only how they put the materials together.

The insects live in the lower, wider parts of the mound. That's where the nest is located and where the queen termite lives. Because the queen never leaves her small chamber, she has to get air or she would die. So, termites build tall openings, or chimneys, that stretch from the chamber to the top of the mound to bring in air and keep the entire mound cool.

The mound stays cool because hot air rises and cool air falls. That means when it's hot, the warm air rises from the chimneys. And when it's cold outside, cool air "falls" into the chimneys. This process causes air to move through the structure like a natural air-conditioning system.

Engineers decided to design buildings and homes that do the same thing. An office building in Zimbabwe was one of the first building complexes to be built similar to a termite mound. The walls are made of concrete, which is porous: The walls have millions of tiny holes that allow air to flow through the concrete. During the day, chimneys in the building bring in air. The concrete walls then absorb the hot air and let cool air flow throughout the rest of the building. At night, cooler air outside the building draws the stored hot air out of the concrete. Unlike a true termite mound, the building does have to add a fan system to keep air moving. However, people who shop and work there are happy with the ventilation system.

▲ AN ECO-FRIENDLY BUILDING INSPIRED BY TERMITES IN ZIMBABWE, AFRICA

# DOLPHIN-INSPIRED TSUNAMI SENSORS

## Amazing Animal
## BOTTLENOSE DOLPHIN

**KNOWN FOR HIGH JUMPS,** stunts, and swimming alongside boats, dolphins are large, aquatic mammals with sleek bodies, fins, and rounded heads. These playful animals have the ability to communicate with one another over long distances.

## DESIGN DILEMMA

**WHEN AN EARTHQUAKE STRIKES** deep in the ocean floor, a dangerous tsunami sometimes follows. A series of giant waves that rush inland, a tsunami swamps everything in its path. One can occur so quickly that it is difficult to give people warning before it strikes. Tsunamis can cause massive destruction to land, buildings, and people. More than 60,000 people are affected by this force of nature every year. How can we do a better job of warning people when one might happen?

▲ TSUNAMIS CAN DEVASTATE COASTAL AREAS.

Tsunami warning systems have been in place since 1940, but they have not always been accurate. Sending a long-distance signal through the ocean is difficult. The signals can sometimes be interrupted and not reach their destination. Timing is extremely important in a tsunami warning, but engineers were stumped ... until dolphins provided inspiration.

Dolphins can "talk" to other dolphins that are more than 12 miles (20 km) away. Because sound waves bend and scatter in water, engineers wanted to learn more.

## BUILDING BIONICS

**DOLPHINS COMMUNICATE BY** making a clicking noise from their larynx (an area below their blowholes) and sending that sound through the water on multiple frequencies, which work like channels on a television. When you change the channel, you change the frequency. Dolphins tend to use low-frequency sounds to communicate, and they use high frequencies for echolocation. Unlike separate TV channels that we use, dolphins can hear all the frequencies at once and choose which ones to focus on.

A team of engineers thought: Why can't we do that with sensors in the ocean? So, they created waterproof sensors shaped like small cylinders with antennae that record earthquakes and send out signals at different frequencies—just like dolphin communication. This increased the chances that the signals would be received, and that they wouldn't interfere with one another. These sensors can also be used to transmit information to ships so they can be alerted about incoming tsunamis.

▼ ACOUSTIC SENSORS PLACED UNDERWATER WARN OF AN APPROACHING TSUNAMI.

## GOING **FURTHER**

Where is the **BEST PLACE** for **SOUND TO TRAVEL?** An area of the ocean roughly **1,094 YARDS** (1,000 m) **DEEP** known as the **SOFAR** (**SOUND FIXING AND RANGING CHANNEL**). In this area, sound waves can travel **THOUSANDS OF MILES** without losing the signal.

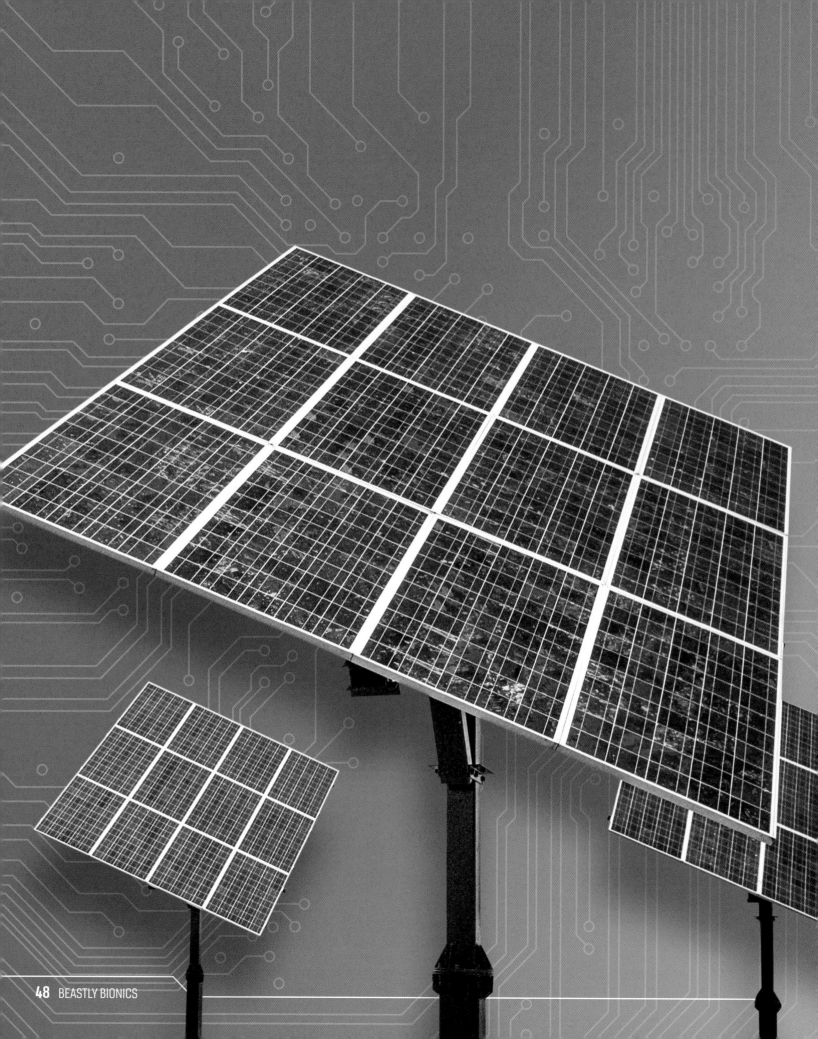

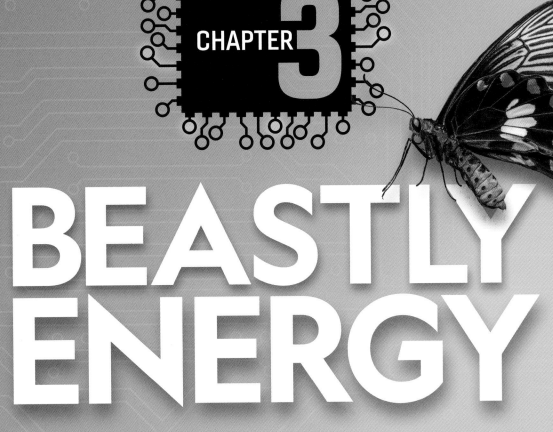

# CHAPTER 3

# BEASTLY ENERGY

▶YAHOO! IT'S A SNOW DAY! You've been out sliding on your favorite sledding hill all afternoon. But now your fingers and toes are turning into icicles. Time to race home, crank up the heat, and slurp down some hot chocolate. A warm home is awesome, but wouldn't it be better if that heat were produced using eco-friendly energy? Biomimetics can help with that.

Think of how much energy your house uses. It's a lot. Solar panels on your house can help. If they could store all of the energy they collect and turn it into usable electricity, you wouldn't need power lines at all. The problem: Solar energy technology is not yet as efficient as using fossil fuels.

But that's rapidly changing, thanks in part to the rose butterfly and biomimetic research. This chapter is packed with ways to improve energy efficiency by mimicking whales and owls in wind turbine design, using water-capturing technology modeled after beetles, making cement inspired by coral, and more.

Most **BUTTERFLIES** live for about a month. A few species, such as the monarch butterfly, can live for nine months or more.

## GOING **FURTHER**

At present, **SOLAR PANELS** must sit at a **CERTAIN ANGLE** to absorb the most sunlight. And some panels need to move as the sun does throughout the day, which **REQUIRES ENERGY.** If in the future such panels are made out of a **BUTTERFLY-INSPIRED MATERIAL,** they would able to **ABSORB SUNLIGHT** from any angle. **NO MOVING REQUIRED!** That's just one more way these **BIOMIMETIC SOLAR PANELS** will save energy.

# SOLAR-POWERED BUTTERFLIES

## Amazing Animal
## ROSE BUTTERFLY

**FOUND IN SOUTHEAST ASIA,** this large, black-winged insect needs sunlight to fly. Its wing structures allow it to absorb sunlight at any angle.

## DESIGN DILEMMA

**ENGINEERS AND SCIENTISTS** have been working on ways to capture solar power—energy from the sun—to use in our everyday lives. Why? Solar power is renewable, which means it will never run out as long as the sun shines. Solar power is also much better for the environment. So why isn't solar power used everywhere?

Today's solar panels are made up of special sun-attracting objects, called photovoltaic cells, that absorb energy from the sun's rays and turn it into electricity. These are quite expensive. Thin film solar cells are also used, but they're not very efficient, so they're usually used in watches and calculators. This brings us to the rose butterfly, specifically, its wings.

## BUILDING BIONICS

**THE ROSE BUTTERFLY IS COLD-BLOODED,** meaning that its body can't generate its own heat. Instead, it absorbs sunlight through its black wings for energy to fly. But how exactly does this work?

The wings are made up of hundreds of tiny scales stacked partially on top of one another, kind of how roof shingles overlap. The scales have tiny holes (a teeny-tiny fraction of an inch—about one ten-thousandth of a centimeter—in size), where the heat most likely seeps into the butterfly's body to keep it warm. Engineers determined that these openings allow for sunlight to scatter evenly across the wings.

Building on this idea, engineers attached extremely thin sheets of silicon to a solar panel and added tiny holes on both sides of them, just like those on the butterfly's wings. They wanted to see if the heat would travel to the panels underneath. It worked! These panels absorbed heat much more quickly than the regular solar panels did. Maybe someday you will see solar panels like these on your own roof.

▲ THE ROSE BUTTERFLY HAS SCALES THAT ABSORB THE SUN'S RAYS, JUST LIKE THE TINY HOLES IN A SOLAR PANEL.

# SILENT SWOOPERS

## Amazing Animal OWLS

**THESE BEAUTIFUL AND MAJESTIC BIRDS** soar silently through the night in search of prey. Their wings are uniquely shaped and have feathers on the edges, which allows air to pass through with only a small whooshing sound.

## DESIGN DILEMMA

**IF YOU'VE EVER** had a fan running in your house, you know how loud it can be. And the faster a fan runs, the louder it is. Imagine if that fan were outside and even louder. It would bother people and animals living in the area.

This is the problem with giant wind turbines—the huge, white, fan-like structures you may have seen as part of a hilltop wind farm. These turbines use wind to generate a renewable and efficient source of electricity. The problem is that the rotors—the parts with the spinning blades—make a lot of noise when they turn. Studies have shown that this noise can disturb animals' mating habits and their communication, and even cause them to leave an area. But how do you make a giant fan quieter? Ask an owl.

▼ WIND FARMS CAN SUPPLY 1,500 HOMES A YEAR WITH ECO-FRIENDLY ENERGY.

## BUILDING BIONICS

**HOW DO OWLS SWOOP** so quietly through the sky? They have special feathers with two features that make their flights extra quiet. The edges of the feathers are very rough, kind of like a bristly hairbrush. They break up sound waves as the wings cut through air, preventing the air from making noise as it rushes over the wings. The upper surface of each wing is made of a downy material that's as soft as a cotton ball. The soft feathers reduce the air pressure by spreading it out. That also muffles the sound.

Scientists imitated the owl's rough bristles by putting fins on the front and back of a turbine's giant fan blades. Then they tested it in a wind tunnel. The result? The fins cut the noise by a factor of 10. Now the blades can run faster and more quietly. And the animals and people living nearby greatly appreciate this wise move.

▲ ROUGH FEATHERS ON THE EDGE OF THE WING BREAK UP SOUND WAVES, REDUCING NOISE.

## GOING FURTHER

NOISE POLLUTION is a serious issue. If you live in a city, you hear the sound of CONSTANT TRAFFIC, PEOPLE LOADING AND UNLOADING SUPPLY TRUCKS, CONSTRUCTION, AND MORE. All of these contribute to noise pollution, which can have a NEGATIVE EFFECT ON PEOPLE. It can cause them to LOSE THEIR FOCUS AND LOSE SLEEP. The same thing can happen to ANIMALS that live in or near cities. Changing the design of WIND TURBINES has helped engineers to consider other ways to reduce all kinds of noise pollution.

# WINDY WHALE

**D**R. FRANK E. FISH, an expert in animal biomechanics at West Chester University in Pennsylvania, U.S.A., was browsing in a gift shop when a sculpture of a humpback whale caught his eye. The sculpture had tubercles, or bumps, on what he believed to be the leading edges—the edges on the front of the flippers. He was puzzled. He hadn't known that whales had tubercles there. Had the artist added them? He asked the store owner to show him a picture of a humpback.

Dr. Fish discovered that, yes, a humpback whale does indeed have tubercles on the edge of its flippers. This led him to a great discovery about energy-efficient wind turbines. As a humpback whale swims through the deep ocean, it uses its tail flukes and massive, bumpy, yet aerodynamic flippers to propel itself through the water. Because gliding through water is similar to moving through air, the whale's flippers are the perfect inspiration for an airplane wing or wind turbine blade.

You might think a turbine blade should be long, sort of triangular, and flat. Not exactly. The most efficient turbine blades are not flat at all. A blade has two mechanical forces acting on it when it spins in the air: lift and drag. Lift occurs when a solid object moves through air or water. As the blade moves, the force of lift pushes the blade upward. The larger the force of lift, the easier the blade moves through the air. Drag is also a factor. While the blade is moving up, drag is pulling it back. The drag force is the opposite of the direction of movement. Think of it as friction in the water. Drag slows the blade down, which means more energy is required to keep it moving.

What Dr. Fish realized was that the fin of a humpback whale and a blade on a wind turbine are basically acting in the same manner, with the fin cutting through water and the blade through air. The tubercles on the whale flipper increase lift and reduce drag so the whale uses less energy while it swims. Dr. Fish took some inspiration from the whale and applied it to wind turbine blades—and it worked!

◄ THE TUBERCLES, OR BUMPY RIDGES, ON THE EDGES OF A WIND TURBINE BLADE MAKE THE BLADES GLIDE THROUGH THE AIR AS EASILY AS A WHALE SWIMS.

**HOW DO THE TUBERCLES HELP** with the problem of the blades? A flat blade turning at a steep angle increases drag, making the blade go slower. Enter the *flipper-spiration!* Engineers added tubercles to the edges of their wind turbine blades. This caused the blades to cut through air at a much steeper angle. These new "bumpy" blades reduced the drag by about a third and increased lift by 8 percent. Talk about energy efficient!

# FIREFLY LIGHTBULBS

## Amazing Animal
## FIREFLY (OR LIGHTNING BUG)

**THIS FLYING BEETLE** could be mistaken for a regular fly, except it has a flashing light built onto its abdomen. Most fireflies in the United States are only found east of the Rocky Mountains.

## DESIGN DILEMMA

**TODAY'S LIGHTBULBS** are usually made of light-emitting diodes (LEDs), which are energy efficient and cool to the touch. An LED bulb can also typically last up to 10 years after purchase. An LED bulb contains a tiny diode—an electronic device that allows electricity to pass through it. This generates light, which then passes through the bulb and illuminates your room.

But early LED lights had a problem. The light would get stuck inside the bulb and reflect back at the light source, the diode, making the bulb seem dim. Engineers knew they needed to fix this if LEDs were ever going to be useful. Good thing they found a fix, with a little help from the firefly.

## GOING **FURTHER**

**LIGHTBULBS** have come a long way since they were **INVENTED BACK IN THE 1800s.** Originally, they had a tiny piece of bent wire, called a **FILAMENT,** inside a glass bulb. When an **ELECTRIC CURRENT** moved through the filament, it **LIT UP,** producing light. The problem was that the filament also got **VERY HOT** while it was illuminated. At first, the filament would burn out rather quickly. Over the years, engineers improved the lightbulb by making the filaments **LAST LONGER.** Eventually, **LEDs WERE CREATED,** and they were so **EFFICIENT** that the old incandescent bulb has pretty much become a thing of the past.

▼ORIGINAL INCANDESCENT LIGHTBULB DESIGNED BY THOMAS EDISON

THOMAS A. EDISON
ELECTRIC-LAMP
No. 223,898   Pat'd Jan. 27, 1880

## BUILDING BIONICS

**FIREFLIES ARE BIOLUMINESCENT** insects, which means they are living organisms that give off light. A firefly creates light through a chemical reaction in a light organ on its stomach. It can control when the light turns on and off by adding oxygen from the air. Most lights give off heat due to a chemical process, but a firefly's light is cold. The light also shines quite bright, while using little energy. That's because a firefly has many tiny, jagged scales on its outer skeleton. The light reflects off these scales and releases a bright glow. The same thing happens if you shine a light on a diamond. It reflects back bright light that makes a disco ball pattern.

Scientists thought that if they could re-create that pattern within an LED bulb, they might be able to increase its efficiency. Several teams came up with different patterns. One used jagged scales on an LED bulb. This produced 55 percent more brightness than a normal LED. Another team used three different layers. The top layer is made of reflective material that functions like the firefly's skeleton. The middle layer is the normal diode, and the bottom layer is an aluminum reflector. The result was a 60 percent increase in brightness. The three layers work together to focus the light to make it brighter and more efficient than the original bulb, too. You could say that in this case, biomimicry is shining a light on technology and efficiency.

▲ TINY LED BULBS PROVIDE BRIGHT LIGHT EFFICIENTLY.

# IN-SYNC GEESE

## Amazing Animal
## CANADA GOOSE

**THE CANADA GOOSE** is a large bird that flies in a flock in a V-formation. They fly between 2,000 and 3,000 miles (3,200 to 4,800 km) when they are migrate south during the fall.

## DESIGN DILEMMA

**EVERY DAY,** thousands of planes fly across the skies, moving machinery, packages, and people to distant places. All of these planes use a lot of fuel. Companies are always looking for ways to make flying more efficient so that planes use less fuel, take less time, and have less of an impact on the environment. Engineers have spent many hours searching for solutions. It's kind of funny, but all they had to do was to look to the sky. Canada geese have a special way of traveling that is extremely efficient.

▼ SOMEDAY, DRONES LIKE THESE MIGHT DELIVER PACKAGES TO YOU.

### HELPFUL ADDITIONS
Researchers are studying how the V-formation could perhaps be used for multiple drones— tiny, remote-controlled air- craft—to drop off packages along a similar flight path.

## BUILDING BIONICS

**WHEN FLOCKS OF** Canada geese take to the sky, one bird leads and the rest spread out like a V behind it. Throughout the flight, the birds take turns flying in the lead position.

Engineers wanted to know why geese fly like that. Is there a benefit to keeping this V shape? It turns out there is. When the first bird is flying, its wing movements push the air behind it in swirl shapes. If the other geese are in range of the swirls, the air lifts them a little, giv- ing them an extra push. This means that they require less of their own energy to stay in the air. So each bird in the V makes it easier for the bird behind it to fly.

Now consider if planes flew in this formation. The lead plane would create the same swirls of air that could provide lift to an airplane behind it. Energy saved over long distances could save a lot of fuel.

Airlines, specifically ones that carry packages and cargo on a regular basis, are working to create computer programs that would keep planes steady within a V-formation. They would do this by using the autopilot system. A V-formation of multiple planes would not work for passenger airlines because they fly different routes rather than all traveling to the same place, and they wouldn't be able to safely fly that close together. However, one day you may look up and see planes flying in a V shape, just like birds!

▼ CANADIAN GEESE FLYING IN V-FORMATION

## GOING **FURTHER**

**SPEED SKATERS, RACE CAR DRIVERS, AND SURFERS** use a technique similar to that of the Canada goose. It's called **"DRAFTING"** for cars or skaters and **"WAKE-SURFING"** for surfers. They don't make a V-formation, but racers will often cruise along behind a leader, taking advantage of the lead's **"WAKE"** to save energy. If the leader slows or gets tired, the person following them can **PASS AND WIN THE RACE!**

# FOG-CAPTURING BEETLES

## Amazing Animal
## NAMIB DESERT BEETLE

**THIS LEGGY INSECT HAS A SMALL,** round body and lives mostly in the sand dunes of Africa's Namib Desert. How does it survive these extreme conditions? It has the amazing ability to capture water for drinking on its back.

## DESIGN DILEMMA

**WATER IS THE MOST IMPORTANT THING** that humans need to survive. What happens if you live where water is scarce? You can transport it via pipes, but that is expensive and takes a lot of energy. Or you can try to get water from the air. But collecting water that way is time-consuming and also takes a lot of energy. And if there is little or no rain, you won't get any water.

The best way to get water every day is to collect the morning fog or dew. When the temperature on the ground is colder than the air, condensation takes place. This means that water turns from a vapor (a gas floating in the air) into a liquid. That's what causes the small drops of moisture, or dew, that appear on rocks, plants, and bushes. This freshwater is clean and great for drinking. If only humans could capture it like some beetles can!

### HELPFUL ADDITIONS

Researchers may also use the beetle as a model for rooftop water collection systems in the desert. This would require very little energy to collect water.

▶ BUMPS ON THE BACK OF THIS NAMIB DESERT BEETLE HELP COLLECT DEW DROPS.

## BUILDING BIONICS

THE NAMIB BEETLE has bumps across its back that attract water—one of nature's amazing innovations. When morning fog—filled with millions of drops of water vapor—comes into contact with these bumps, water particles stick to the bumps. Small drops of moisture form on the beetle's back. The bumps are surrounded by hydrophobic— or water-repelling—sections, which send the liquid down the shell and right into the beetle's mouth. Nice catch!

Figuring out how to mimic this action is a tough task, to say the least. Early attempts by engineers at creating a combined hydrophilic (water-attracting) and hydrophobic (water-repelling) material did not work. They relied on multilayered designs that were extremely expensive. But a team of scientists in Thuwal, Saudi Arabia, were able to create a similar material with an ink-jet printer. They made the bumps using a special hydrophilic fluid, and then they printed the pattern of bumps on chemically treated, hydrophobic paper. The result was similar to what happens on the beetle shell. The material worked to harvest a small amount of water. Although scientists are still researching ways to collect water on a large scale, this technology is a promising first step.

▲ A SCIENTIST INSPECTS A FOG COLLECTION SYSTEM IN THE ATACAMA DESERT.

## GOING FURTHER

A PHYSICS PROFESSOR in Chile has developed FOG-CATCHING NETS and is testing them in some of the driest regions of his country. These nets have openings that are less than .04 inch (1 mm), which TRAP WATER MOLECULES as they condense. When multiple drops are gathered, their combined weight is enough to run down the net and into the attached water tank. This method is MUCH CHEAPER than using pipes to bring water into buildings and houses.

# CORAL-INSPIRED CEMENT

## Amazing Animal CORAL

**CORAL MAY LOOK MORE LIKE** a funky rock than an animal, but it is very much alive. These tiny ocean organisms, called polyps, join together to form huge coral reefs. Polyps are surrounded by a hard and sturdy material, which forms a reef. Reefs are home to millions of other sea animals.

## DESIGN DILEMMA

**THE MATERIALS USED TO BUILD HOUSES,** schools, shopping malls, and skyscrapers are not always good for the environment. That's because the energy needed to make bricks, steel, and concrete often comes from fossil fuels such as coal, natural gas, or oil. These fossil fuels give off gases—like carbon dioxide and methane—that can harm the environment. When these gases build up, the atmosphere traps heat, which causes a rise in temperatures on Earth. This, in turn, results in an overall warming of the planet, which affects every living organism. But could new buildings be created without releasing harmful carbon dioxide into the atmosphere?

Engineers wanted to know. They started studying whether they could make a building material that would trap and hold excess carbon dioxide permanently. They realized that coral could help with that.

▼ BERGERON CENTRE AT YORK UNIVERSITY, A PLACE FOR GROUNDBREAKING ECOLOGICAL ENGINEERING

## BUILDING BIONICS

**WHEN CARBON DIOXIDE** enters water, it dissolves and either stays in that form or becomes carbonic acid. This acid sometimes breaks down further into a salt called carbonate. Coral mixes the carbonate with calcium, a type of mineral, to build more coral. During this process, the coral absorbs the carbon dioxide. Engineers wanted to copy this process when creating cement.

Cement is made by heating limestone, a form of calcium carbonate, to extremely high temperatures—around 2640°F (1449°C)! The energy to heat the limestone usually comes from burning fossil fuels. Now some companies have figured out how to capture the carbon dioxide that these processes create, and then, before the concrete hardens, inject the carbon dioxide back into the concrete. Instead of releasing the toxic carbon dioxide into the atmosphere, the concrete recycles its own waste, just as coral does.

In 2017, the process of making concrete released approximately four billion pounds (1.8 billion kg) of carbon dioxide into the atmosphere. With this new technique, one concrete company estimates that it has prevented at least 10 million pounds (4.5 million kg) of carbon dioxide from entering the atmosphere since 2016. These promising results are something to cheer about!

## GOING **FURTHER**

CARBON DIOXIDE is a gas found everywhere in the world. But today, HUMANS ARE PRODUCING MORE carbon dioxide than ever before. This carbon dioxide, along with the other GREENHOUSES GASES, is causing our planet to get warmer. THE OCEAN CAN HELP WITH THAT: It is a "CARBON SINK," which means that carbon dioxide IS ABSORBED by the ocean as part of the CARBON CYCLE. The carbon is BROKEN DOWN INTO FOOD for some organisms, becomes PART OF THE SHELLS of others, or is STORED INSIDE LIMESTONE formed from shells that CEMENTED TOGETHER over time. Although this process is one of NATURE'S GREAT SUCCESSES, the ocean cannot absorb all the carbon dioxide produced today. And excessive levels of carbon dioxide make the ocean MORE ACIDIC and less healthy.

# SHIPSHAPE PENGUINS

## Amazing Animal
## EMPEROR PENGUINS

**THESE "TUXEDO-**wearing" birds are the world's largest penguins at about 3 feet 9 inches tall (1.2 m). When they're underwater, they can shoot through water like a torpedo, diving as deep as 1,850 feet (564 m)!

## DESIGN DILEMMA

**A SHIP NEEDS FUEL TO KEEP MOVING THROUGH WATER.** When the tank starts running low out on the ocean, a ship can't exactly fill up at a local gas station. Instead, the gas station comes to it. A barge carrying fuel pulls up alongside it. Both boats must keep moving at the same speed so that the waves don't push them into each other. The barge uses a long hose to pump gas into the ship's tank. This, of course, means that both the ship and the barge are using a lot of gas.

Burning fuel just to refuel hardly makes sense. So, how can a ship use less gas in the first place? The biggest drain on fuel efficiency is called drag, or the force that pushes back on a ship as it moves through the water. Our friend, the emperor penguin, may be able to help make drag, well, less of a drag.

▼ A CARGO SHIP CARRIES GOODS ACROSS THE OCEAN IN LARGE SHIPPING CONTAINERS.

## BUILDING BIONICS

EMPEROR PENGUINS are great swimmers. But one of the coolest things they can do is launch themselves out of the water and land with a slip-sliding belly flop on an iceberg. Penguins may be birds, but they can't actually fly. Yet they burst out of the water as if they have tiny rockets under their wings! So, what's their secret? When a penguin is ready to leave the water, it swims near the surface, moving its wings back and forth slightly. This traps air between its body and wings. Then it dives down to about 50 to 65 feet (15 to 20 m). During the dive, the penguin presses its wings against its body, pushing out air as tiny bubbles. The bubbles spread out and form a layer of air around the bird's body, making it go faster as it heads back to the surface. Then, pop! The penguin propels itself onto the ice. How can this launching movement help ships? The layer of bubbles against the penguin's body reduces its drag through the water. Maybe a layer of bubbles around a ship could do the same thing. Scientists tried shooting a stream of bubbles around the hull—the body of a ship—as it moved through the water. They did see a tiny improvement in fuel efficiency. And who knows what the future holds? With more testing and new technology, we may have more efficient ships that glide through the water on a carpet of air.

▲ AN EMPEROR PENGUIN PREPARES TO LAUNCH FROM THE SEA ONTO THE SEA ICE.

## GOING FURTHER

To use TRAPPED AIR to increase a ship's speed and EFFICIENCY, scientists have also considered building a SHIP'S HULL with an INDENTATION and then PUMPING AIR into that space. This would create a layer of air between the hull and the ship just like the STREAM OF BUBBLES along the NATURAL HULL. Both processes would REDUCE DRAG and make the ship GO FASTER WHILE USING LESS FUEL.

# SHARKSKIN SUPERPOWERS

**W**HEN YOU THINK OF A SHARK, you might imagine its sleek body cutting through water with impressive speed. A shark's skin has a lot to do with this awesome skill. And it's one of the most valuable opportunities for biomimicry.

Sharkskin may look smooth, but it's actually made up of tiny overlapping scales called denticles. These break up water as it flows over the skin, sending the water around the tip of a scale—like the way a ship's bow pushes water out of the way as the ship moves forward. This reduces drag—the force of the water pushing back—and allows the shark to zoom through water at a superfast speed. Check out some of the ways sharkskin has helped people, including reducing drag on swimmers and cars, and even resisting bacteria!

▶ THE MAKO SHARK GLIDES EFFORTLESSLY JUST UNDER THE SURFACE OF THE OCEAN.

## RESISTING BACTERIA

The cool thing about **SHARKSKIN DENTICLES** is that they not only **INCREASE SPEED, THEY ALSO PREVENT BACTERIA FROM GROWING.** The denticles stop water from collecting behind a shark's scales, and **BACTERIA CAN'T GROW WITHOUT WATER.** That can be **REALLY USEFUL IN HOSPITALS,** which are always working to **PREVENT THE SPREAD OF DISEASE AND INFECTION.** A company has created a material that's **PATTERNED LIKE DENTICLES.** It has **MICROSCOPIC RIDGES** that decrease bacterial growth by **PREVENTING BACTERIA** from attaching and spreading. The idea is to **SPRAY IT ON COUNTERS** and **OTHER FLAT SURFACES** to see if it **PREVENTS** bacteria growth. It's a **REVOLUTIONARY IDEA,** and one that may reduce the **REINFECTION RATES** at hospitals.

## FAST SWIMMERS

**WISH YOU COULD SWIM AS FAST AS A SHARK? SO DO COMPETITIVE SWIMMERS!** The swimsuits designed for **OLYMPIC SWIMMERS** were inspired by sharkskin. The designers added **TINY DENTICLES** to the suits to help **REDUCE DRAG** in the water. The swimsuits appeared to work. More than 80 percent of the **SWIMMING MEDALS** awarded during the 2000 Sydney Olympics went to athletes who wore the suits. In 2009, an updated version of the swimsuit and similar models were banned from events for providing too much of an **ADVANTAGE** over other suits. The thing is, the denticles didn't contribute to the swimmers' success. Instead, the tight-fitting suits made the Olympians' bodies **MORE COMPACT,** which helped reduce drag.

## ENERGY-EFFICIENT CARS

**SHARKSKIN TECHNOLOGY** may also **DECREASE DRAG ON CARS.** As a car moves, air flows around it and **CREATES TURBULENCE**—waves of air behind the car. This slows the car. Engineers have developed a **SHARKSKIN-LIKE COATING** called a **VORTEX GENERATOR** that wraps around the entire outside of a vehicle. The coating has tiny ridges, **LIKE DENTICLES,** that break up the airflow and reduce drag, making the car **FASTER AND MORE ENERGY EFFICIENT.** Although the research is still pending on exactly how much the ridges can reduce drag and **IMPROVE AERODYNAMICS,** it is certainly an interesting possibility.

# CHAPTER 4

# BEASTLY HEALERS

▶ **YOU AND A FRIEND** are out on a hike. Suddenly, you trip and fall to the ground. Clearly, you didn't see the big root sticking out of the ground in front of you. You stand up and brush yourself off, but then realize that you have cut your knee. It's a pretty deep cut, and blood is gushing out. You apply pressure to stop the bleeding.

Your friend rummages through her backpack, looking for first aid supplies. She pulls out a flexible blue bandage. It's a little strange-looking—it is kind of soft and rubbery—but you put it on your knee anyway. Your cut is very deep, and you might need stitches. You give it a try. To your surprise, the bandage covers the wound and the bleeding stops. Not only that, you don't have to walk stiffly. You can bend and flex your knee to easily walk back to camp. Your knee isn't even that painful. Did your friend hand you a bandage with super-healing powers? Sort of. Would you believe the bandage is modeled after slug slime? With its ability to stick to wet skin, hold tightly, and stretch without breaking, the bandage is unlike any other.

Although you can't buy these bandages yet, they may be one of the many animal-inspired medical creations available in the future. Take a look at the amazing ways the biomimetic inventions in this chapter, such as sunscreen inspired by hippos and a prosthetic arm modeled after an octopus, can heal and protect the human body.

▼ A SLOW-MOVING SLUG CREEPS ACROSS A TREE, LEAVING BEHIND A STICKY TRAIL.

## GOING **FURTHER**

**SLUG-INSPIRED BANDAGES** have so much **POTENTIAL.** If they could **STOP HEAVY BLEEDING,** they could **SAVE PEOPLE'S LIVES.** They might also be useful for **DELIVERING MEDICINES VIA A WATERPROOF PATCH.** You'll never look at a **SLIPPERY SLUG** the same way again.

# SLUG SURGICAL GLUE

## Amazing Animal
### SLUG

**THIS SLOW-MOVING CREEPY CRAWLER** leaves a trail of slime (actually, mucus!) wherever it goes. When startled or threatened, the slug attaches itself to an object and is extremely tough to remove.

## DESIGN DILEMMA

**FINDING A WAY TO HEAL WOUNDS** is a huge problem in medicine. It's even more difficult to do inside the body—like after surgery—than on the skin. The human body is a moist place. You can't just put a bandage on the wound. In a wet environment, it would come off. Plus, how would the bandage be removed? It would have to be able to dissolve on its own so that another surgery isn't needed to remove it.

Now, think of a tough place to fix inside the body—the human heart. The heart beats continuously, which means the heart muscle expands and contracts nonstop. Closing a wound on a beating heart is not easy. Any type of cut you make into the heart must be closed with stitches, which don't expand and contract as the heart beats. Stitches sometimes don't hold well and can interfere with the heart's movement. Doctors have been searching for years for something to help. Believe it or not, slug slime may be the answer.

### Did You KNOW?

**SLUGS** are basically snails without a shell. They have green blood (called hemocyanin) and spend most of their lives underground.

## BUILDING BIONICS

**A SLUG MOVES BY SECRETING SLIME FROM ITS FOOT.** (A slug has one foot, and it looks nothing like a human's.) The thick goo oozes out and allows the slug to glide across surfaces. Without it, the slug couldn't move. The slime is made of tiny crystals called "liquid crystals" because they are between a liquid and a solid. The crystals help slugs stick to objects if they want to crawl up or down. When a slug feels threatened, it secretes an extrastrong type of slime that allows the slug to stick to any surface. This comes in handy if a bird spots it and swoops in for a snack. The bird can try to pluck the slug off its perch, but the bird can't grab it and pull it away. The slug survives another day.

Scientists began studying slug slime for its special gripping abilities. They then discovered something even more interesting. Not only does the slime grip tightly, it's also flexible—another very useful quality! Scientists got to work creating an adhesive, tape-like substance based on the makeup of slug slime. They used a lot of water, which is a component of slug slime, and a mucus-like substance produced by algae whose properties are similar to slug slime. When the scientists put these materials together, they had made a bandage that was flexible and strong enough to stick to a pig's beating heart!

The bandage is still being tested, but it could possibly be used to help patients heal more quickly after open-heart surgery. Although it may seem like a strange idea, open-heart surgery patients may one day owe their lives to a tiny slimy slug.

▶ SURGICAL ADHESIVE INSPIRED BY SLUG SLIME (IN BLUE) HOLDS WOUNDS TOGETHER AND HELPS THEM HEAL.

# HEARING-HELPING FLY

## Amazing Animal
## ORMIA OCHRACEA *FLY*

**THIS TINY FLY IS PARASITIC,** meaning it lives on a host animal such as a cricket. It also has extremely good hearing.

## DESIGN DILEMMA

**MORE THAN 5 PERCENT OF THE WORLD'S POPULATION** has hearing loss. It can be very frustrating for people with hearing loss to be unable to hear a doorbell, sounds from a television, or even a family member talking. How can doctors help these people?

Hearing aids have been around for decades, and some work better than others. Their usefulness also depends on the individual. Each person may have a different reason for their hearing loss. Perhaps they were born without the ability to hear. Others may have been injured in an accident or worked around loud machinery that damaged their hearing. In addition, hearing aids amplify all types of sound. That makes it difficult for people to block out background noises, such as cars honking and people talking loudly in restaurants. There must be a better solution.

The *Ormia ochracea* fly may have provided an answer. Despite its small size—only 0.4 inch (1 cm) long, or half the width of a dime—the *Ormia ochracea* fly has a complex auditory (hearing) system. Engineers are studying that system now. If a hearing aid could mimic the fly's hearing system, the way humans hear in the future could change for the better.

▲ IN-EAR HEARING AIDS HELP TO ENHANCE SOUND FOR THE PEOPLE WHO WEAR THEM.

## Did You KNOW?

The **ORMIA OCHRACEA FLY** doesn't use vision to see a cricket. Instead, it uses its excellent hearing to track it.

THE *ORMIA OCHRACEA* FLY has an extremely compact auditory system. Its two ears are only .08 inch (2 mm) apart. But the system works very well. For example, the sound of a cricket chirping enters as vibrations, or back-and-forth movements, in the fly's ear. These vibrations travel through a mechanism like a tiny teeter-totter to the inner ear, which translates the vibrations into an electrical signal. The signal travels to the brain and tells the fly exactly where the cricket is located.

Human ears work in a similar manner, but with one big difference. We hear sounds as vibrations in a straight line. The vibrations are transferred to three tiny bones in the eardrum, called the ossicles, which then send the signal to a part called the cochlea. There, the cochlea transforms the vibration into electrical signals that are sent to the brain.

Scientists determined that the up-and-down motion of the teeter-totter mechanism in its ear is the reason behind the fly's superior hearing. Sound vibrations are transferred more efficiently by this type of movement. So the scientists created a miniature teeter-totter system out of silicon. This allowed the vibrations to travel quickly to a hearing aid's microphone. Then they placed the hearing aid inside a person's ear to amplify, or increase the loudness, of the sound.

The bionic hearing aid is small but powerful. It allows someone to hear people in front of them more clearly, over most background noise. The technology is still being developed, but one day, people might be able to hear like a fly!

### HELPFUL ADDITIONS

The technology from the *Ormia ochracea* fly hearing aids could be used to make tiny microphones for concert performers. These small but powerful mics would block out background noise more effectively than ordinary mics. That's especially important for singers at huge, loud stadium concerts.

# SUNBATHING HIPPO SUNSCREEN

## Amazing Animal
## HIPPOPOTAMUS

**YOU WILL FIND THIS GIGANTIC** land and water creature hanging out at the local watering hole—either next to it or submerged in it. After all, staying cool is a hippo's number one goal.

## DESIGN DILEMMA

**OUCH!** Sunburns can be painful or itchy and can even make you feel a little sick. Everyone knows that using sunscreen can protect their skin. But researchers have discovered that at least two of the chemicals in sunscreen—oxybenzone and octinoxate—may damage coral reefs. What are you supposed to do when you go to the beach? Choose between your skin and coral reefs?

Hold on. There's hope from an unlikely source. It turns out that hippopotamuses can get sunburned just like us. And these animals may have a solution that will keep you from getting fried.

## BUILDING BIONICS

▲ RED MUCUS OOZES OFF A HIPPO.

**HIPPOS SPEND UP** to 16 hours a day underwater, which means they pretty much hide from the sun. When they do surface, they must protect their skin. They do this by secreting a thick red, mucus-like substance to cover their bodies. Scientists analyzed the substance and discovered that it's made up of crystals that scatter light, preventing sunlight from reaching and burning a hippo's skin.

The big question is: How do you turn that substance into something a human can use? Humans can't secrete red mucus from their skin. Instead, scientists began experimenting with different kinds of liquids that contain tiny crystals. Perhaps the hippo "sweat" could be mimicked. Although they are still working on this solution, you may one day wear sunscreen inspired by a hippo. Let's just hope it doesn't make you smell like one! In the meantime, keep wearing your sunscreen—just choose one that's reef safe, too.

SUN SCREEN
SPF 30
SUN PROTECTION CREAM

SUN SCREEN
SPF 10
SUN PROTECTION CREAM

## GOING **FURTHER**

Some people **MISTAKE THE HIPPO'S SECRETION FOR BLOOD,** probably because the **SUBSTANCE** looks **REDDISH** against hippo skin. Scientists think the color may help **ABSORB THE SUN'S ULTRAVIOLET RAYS.** The researchers have also learned that the **RED SUBSTANCE** may act as an **ANTIBIOTIC** as well, helping a hippo **HEAL FROM INJURIES.**

# AWESOME OCTOPUS ARM

## Amazing Animal
## OCTOPUS

**THIS AQUATIC CREATURE** has two flexible "legs" and six bendable "arms" that move, turn, and grasp objects with ease. The six grippers are great for grabbing more than one object at a time or keeping things close while using the two longer limbs for swimming and investigating the environment around them.

## Did You KNOW?

Two-thirds of an **OCTOPUS'S** neurons, or brain cells, are found in the animal's arms. That means an arm can solve problems on its own—such as how to crack open a shellfish. No wonder people think the octopus is one of the smartest animals!

## DESIGN DILEMMA

**CREATING A PROSTHETIC,** or artificial, arm for a person in need is not an easy task. The human arm is an amazing tool. It turns, twists, bends, and has a hand that can do all of these things plus pick up objects. Four fingers and an opposable thumb—meaning the thumb can touch every finger—make a hand great for grasping, holding, and hanging on to things. It's tough to create an artificial arm that can do all of that.

Prosthetic devices, or prostheses, are important tools for people who may have been born without a certain body part or lost a limb due to an accident, injury, or medical condition. With prostheses, people are more able to do daily tasks independently.

But designing these artificial body parts is complicated. It's important to consider the weight of the device, how it works, how much it will cost, and if it's easy to use and comfortable to wear. For help, some engineers have looked to the octopus as a model.

## GOING FURTHER

Every person has **DIFFERENT NEEDS** for their **PROSTHESIS**. Some need **LIMBS THAT ALLOW THEM TO WALK.** Others need to **RUN WITH THEIR PROSTHETIC LIMB.** Engineers are thinking out of the box to come up with **DIFFERENT PROSTHESES** to meet everyone's needs. Prosthetic **RACING BLADES** are **FLEXIBLE** and provide the **BOUNCE** needed for **RUNNING.** They were inspired by **KANGAROOS** and **CHEETAHS.**

## BUILDING BIONICS

**RESEARCHER** Kaylene Kau decided to create her own prosthetic arm based on an octopus arm. An octopus has six very flexible "arms" and two equally flexible legs. They are each made up of soft tissue and muscles that bend and stretch. Each arm is able to curl around an object and grab it in a tight grip. Kau thought an octopus arm would serve as a perfect model for her prosthetic arm. She started by creating a long, plastic tube that narrows to a dull point at the end, sort of like an octopus arm. From the "elbow" to the "hand," sections are cut into the plastic. This allows her prosthetic arm to bend and flex.

A motor controls two cables that stretch along the inside of the prosthetic arm. These cables allow the arm to curl around and grip objects tightly— a definite improvement over earlier prostheses. The octopus arm is still experimental, but one day it might be available for people who need it. High five (or eight) for the octopus!

▼ AN OCTOPUS ARM–SHAPED PROSTHESIS IS VERY USEFUL FOR PICKING UP OBJECTS.

# NEEDLE-NOSE WORMS

## Amazing Animal
## SPINY-HEADED WORM

**THIS TINY, ALMOST MICROSCOPIC WORM** has a super-gripper snout, or nose, that it uses to attach itself to the intestine of an animal.

## DESIGN DILEMMA

**DURING SURGERY,** a doctor must cut through a patient's skin and tissue to get to whatever needs to be fixed inside the body. The problem is, how do you close the cut? Doctors usually use stitches. A stitch is a loop of thread used to hold two sides of an open cut together. It's kind of like using a needle and thread to sew up a hole in your favorite shirt. The main difference is that the thread for stitches is sterile, or germ free. The problem with using stitches is that they need to be tight enough to close the wound, but not so tight that they make the wound wrinkle and leave a scar.

Another way that a doctor can close a wound is to use surgical staples. They are sterile and safe to use on the body. Staples are used when an incision is fairly large and needs to be held in place for a while. Staples can stay in the body up to three weeks. But staples are not flexible, so the patient must be careful when moving around. What is a doctor to do? The spiny-headed worm has just the right part to help.

▲ A NEWLY DESIGNED BANDAGE WITH TINY GRIPPERS TO KEEP IT IN PLACE

## Did You KNOW?

**SPINY-HEADED WORMS** are mostly found in lakes. Although they prefer fish as their hosts, they will also live in amphibians, reptiles, birds, and mammals.

**SPINY-HEADED WORMS** are parasites. That means they cannot live by themselves. A parasite must live inside a host animal, sometimes a fish. The fish becomes the food source for the parasite. A spiny-headed worm uses the tiny needles on its flat, rectangular nose to ram its head into a fish's intestines. The worm then sinks its needles into the intestine's soft tissue and swells to anchor it in place. There the worm sits, absorbing the food it needs from the nutrients the fish flushes into its intestines.

Although this sounds really disgusting, it's actually kind of ingenious. Scientists who have studied the spiny worm got to thinking. They wanted a bandage that would mimic the gripping action of the needles in the spiny-headed worm. Perhaps its needles could be used in place of stitches. Would that be possible? Engineers decided to find out.

▲ THIS BANDAGE, COVERED IN MICRONEEDLES, IS SMALL ENOUGH TO FIT ON A FINGERTIP.

First, scientists created a double-layer adhesive, or tape, to help close wounds and keep the skin in place. The bottom layer is made of microneedles, or extremely small needles, that pierce the skin fairly painlessly and keep it in place. The top layer is made of a material that you might find in diapers, which absorbs liquid and swells to ensure the adhesive sticks. These new adhesives are working so well that they are replacing stitches and other ways of keeping wounds closed. Who knew that a spiny-headed worm could be so helpful to humans?

## GOING FURTHER

People who have **EXTREME BURNS** sometimes need **SKIN GRAFTS.** That's when **HEALTHY SKIN** is taken from another part of their body and **TRANSPLANTED TO THE INJURED AREA.** Using **STITCHES** to keep that new skin in place interferes with the healing process. But this new adhesive, inspired by the **SPINY-HEADED WORM,** could make **HEALING EASIER** for burn victims.

▲ THE TINY SPINY-HEADED WORM USES ITS NEEDLES TO ATTACH ITSELF TO A HOST.

# GECKOS STICK ANYWHERE

**G**ECKOS ARE PRETTY INTERESTING CREATURES. They are lizards that vary greatly in size. Some are a little over a half inch (1.3 cm) long. Others can grow to be more than a foot (30.5 cm) in length. Regardless of their size, all geckos have an awesome ability to stick to practically anything. Although it might seem that geckos have glue on their toes, they actually don't. They do have millions of tiny, nano-size hairs. To give you an idea of how tiny that is, a single strand of human hair is between 60,000 and 100,000 nanometers!

These microscopic hairs grip objects extremely well. About the only surface that a gecko cannot stick to is Teflon because it's too slick. The only way for a gecko to stick to a Teflon pan, such as a cookie sheet, would be to get it wet. The water on the pan provides the tiny bit of friction needed to allow a gecko's feet to stick. With its amazing "stick-to-it-tiveness," the gecko is likely to inspire many biomimetic creations.

## GECKO ADHESIVES

The **GECKO'S STICKY FEET** are inspiring new bandages for humans. These **SUPER-GRIPPY BANDAGES** can be used on both the **INSIDE AND OUTSIDE OF THE BODY.** They stick to wet and dry surfaces and even **FLEX AND BEND WITH YOU.** The bandages are coated with a **SPECIAL TYPE OF GLUE** that contains **THOUSANDS OF MICROSCOPIC GRIPPERS** that stick to the skin. They can also be coated with a substance that will **DELIVER MEDICINES** to the wound.

## UP THE WALL

Wish you could **SCALE BUILDINGS LIKE SPIDER-MAN?** Maybe you can. Scientists are working on making **WALL-CLIMBING PADS** that **ATTACH TO YOUR HANDS AND FEET.** They are designed with **NANO-SIZE FIBERS** and work like the **HAIRS ON A GECKO'S FEET.** The pads attach and pull off the wall easily to allow a climber to keep going using **LESS ENERGY.** It would be great fun to **CLIMB UP TO YOUR CEILING** and **SURVEY THE WORLD** from there, wouldn't it?

## STICKY SPACE TRAVEL

NASA has sent **GECKO GRIPPERS, SMALL FLAT OBJECTS** with the gecko-like **ADHESIVE** attached, to the **INTERNATIONAL SPACE STATION** to see if they can hold things in **MICROGRAVITY**—meaning environments with **LITTLE GRAVITY**. If the adhesive works, astronauts would hope to use the grippers to **ATTACH SENSORS** to satellites both inside the station and outside in **SPACE**.

▲ STICKY PADS ON THE GECKO'S FEET ALLOW IT TO STICK ANYWHERE.

# THE EYES HAVE IT

**G**ECKO EYES ARE UNIQUE! They are one of the few animals on the planet that have only cones, not rods and cones, in their eyes. Rods give you good vision in low light or when it's dark. Cones determine color and also location (distance, height, and so on). Scientists even believe that geckos may be one of the few animals that can see color at night. Scientists are studying gecko eyes to make better cameras and perhaps to improve contact lenses for human eyes.

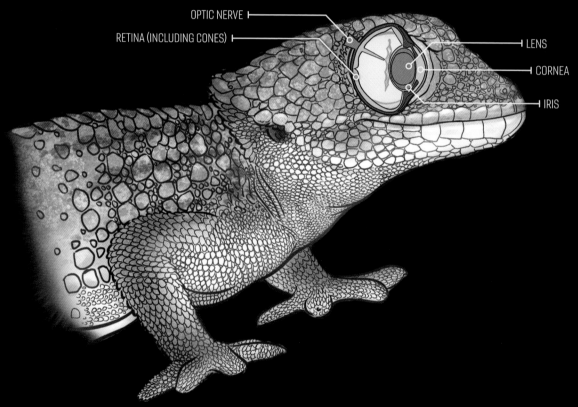

OPTIC NERVE ├

RETINA (INCLUDING CONES) ├

┤ LENS

┤ CORNEA

┤ IRIS

## GECKO AND HUMAN EYES

**CORNEA:** This is a clear dome that sits in front of the iris. This helps the eye focus light.
**LENS:** This sits behind the cornea and focuses light on the back of the eyeball (retina).
**IRIS:** This is the colored part of the eye. It has muscles that change its shape to let a certain amount of light through.
**PUPIL:** This is the black part of the eye, which expands and contracts in response to light.
**RETINA:** This receives the light image and turns it into nerve signals that are sent to the optic nerve.
**OPTIC NERVE:** This sends the nerve signals information from the retina to the brain.
**CONES:** These are located in the retina in the back of the eyeball. Their job is to sense color.

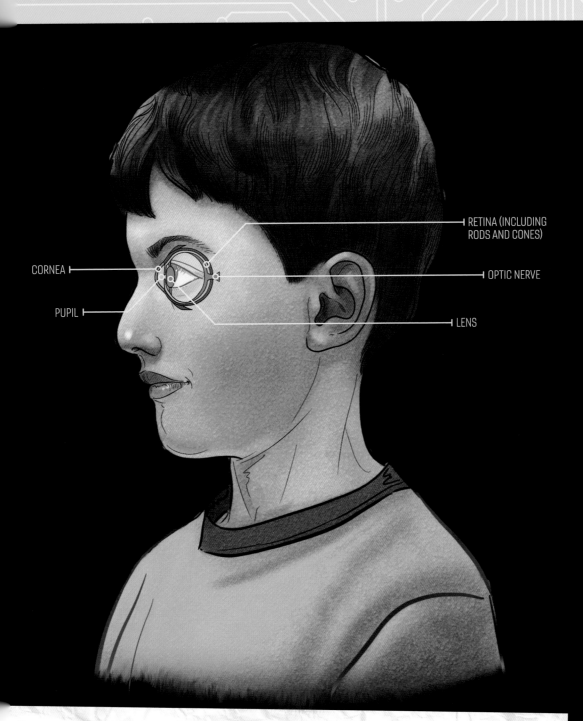

CORNEA

PUPIL

RETINA (INCLUDING RODS AND CONES)

OPTIC NERVE

LENS

## SEEING AT NIGHT

Geckos have large eyes and pupils that open very wide at night to capture any light that is there. This allows them to see very well at night, which is helpful because that is when the geckos, which are nocturnal, need to hunt. Geckos also have multifocal lenses, which means they can see light at different wavelengths in different parts of the lens. This allows the geckos to see color much more clearly than humans, especially at night.

# WORM BONE REPAIR

## Amazing Animal
## SANDCASTLE WORM

**THIS SMALL, BROWN WORM** is no more than three inches (7.6 cm) long. It has purple tentacles and spends its life building tiny, honeycomb-shaped sand structures on rocky beaches. Scientists study the worm in particular for the superstrong material that oozes from its body and is used to build the sand structures.

## DESIGN DILEMMA

**HAVE YOU EVER BROKEN A BONE?** If it was a really bad break, you might have needed surgery. Surgeons may have used pins or screws and plates to put bones back in place. If they did, the recovery process may have been long and painful. Healing probably took weeks or months. The plates, screws, and pins are sometimes in your body for the rest of your life.

Wouldn't it be nice if bones could be fixed without painful surgery? That might be possible one day, thanks to the sandcastle worm.

▼ PUTTING A CAST ON A BROKEN LEG IS EASIER TO DO WITH A BONE-REPAIRING GLUE.

## BUILDING BIONICS

**THE SANDCASTLE WORM** creates its own home to live in. It uses a glue-like substance to stick bits of sand together to make a honeycomb structure—sort of like a beehive. The cool thing is that the glue doesn't dissolve in water. Although the glue comes out of the worm as a gel-like substance, it hardens almost immediately and becomes super strong.

A glue that doesn't dissolve in seawater would be perfect for keeping bones together in the moist environment inside the human body. Plus, the structure of the honeycomb sandcastle is similar to the structure of a human bone. Human bones are not solid throughout. They have a hard outside but a softer inside filled with marrow, which keeps the bones strong. Scientists have developed a glue similar to the sandcastle worm's glue and are testing it on cow bones. It's working well so far. Maybe one day, doctors might be able to glue broken wrists, ankles, and other bones back together instead of doing surgery.

### HELPFUL ADDITIONS

The glue inspired by the sandcastle worm may also be used to glue teeth back together one day. And why not? The wet environment of your mouth is similar in some ways to the ocean: There is a lot of movement, and water is continually flowing through it (as it does when you're swallowing). Just sit down, glue, and go!

The **SANDCASTLE WORM'S** purple tentacles are covered with cilia, or tiny hairs, that are attached to its mouth. It uses these tentacles to sift through particles that float by and pick out the ones it wants to eat.

## GOING **FURTHER**

Will the glue stay **INSIDE A HUMAN BONE FOREVER?** Scientists say no. It may eventually **DISSOLVE** once the **BONE HEALS COMPLETELY.** The glue could also **DELIVER ANTIBIOTICS** or **PAIN RELIEVERS** to the area to **HELP PATIENTS RECOVER MORE QUICKLY.**

# BACTERIA-FIGHTING CICADA

## Amazing Animal
## CLANGER CICADA

**THIS BULKY INSECT,** like most cicadas, sings loudly, but that is not why it's useful to scientists. Its clear wings contain special structures that prevent bacteria from forming.

## DESIGN DILEMMA

**BACTERIA ARE SINGLE-CELLED ORGANISMS** that are found everywhere. They are too small to be seen without a microscope and are found on many different surfaces, including toilet seats, door handles, stair railings, cell phones, and even video game consoles.

Some bacteria are good for you. For example, you have bacteria in your intestines that help break down your food. "Bad" bacteria are anything that might make you sick; for example *Streptococcus* can give you strep throat. Or, if you have an open cut, bacteria can get inside your body and make you sick. This is especially a problem for someone who has a weak immune system and is unable to fight off illness. Because you encounter many types of bacteria in your daily activities, it's important to wash your hands with soap, which removes extra bacteria.

It's very difficult, however, to avoid touching surfaces in public. It would be so much better if bacteria didn't grow on surfaces in the first place. That may be possible one day, thanks to a cicada's tiny wings.

### HELPFUL ADDITIONS
The U.S. Navy is trying to mimic cicada sound and use it for ship-to-ship communications and remote sensing on missions in the future.

Some people eat **CICADAS.** They are good baked, broiled, barbecued, sautéed, or mixed with a tasty sauce. They are also fantastic sources of protein.

## BUILDING BIONICS

**CICADAS' WINGS ARE OVAL-SHAPED** and sweep back and up. When you think of a cicada's wings, you probably remember that they are the reason cicadas make noise at night. But it's not the sound that scientists are interested in.

The cicada's most important biomimetic feature is that their wings kill bacteria on contact. The microscopic ridges on the wings prevent the bacteria from settling there. Here's how it works: A bacterium that lands on the tiny ridge is flexible enough that it stretches and bends. Imagine a balloon resting on a bunch of spikes. The balloon bends down around the spike. But if the wind blows the balloon or someone pushes on it, the spike will stretch the balloon to the breaking point. Pop! The same thing happens to the bacterium. Eventually, its membrane, or skin, breaks apart, killing the bacterium.

Scientists are working to create a substance that can be used in public places—perhaps in bathrooms and on handrails, for example. Someday we may not have to worry about bacteria on surfaces. But, for now, keep washing those hands!

◀ A BACTERIUM BALANCES ON TOP OF THE MICROSCOPIC RIDGES OF A CICADA'S WING.

# CANCER-BUSTING JELLYFISH

## Amazing Animal
### JELLYFISH

**THESE SOFT, BLOBLIKE CREATURES** drift through the ocean with tentacles trailing behind them. Some come in bright colors and are bioluminescent, which means they glow.

## DESIGN DILEMMA

**ONE OF THE MOST** difficult diseases to track inside the body is cancer. The disease happens when cells grow in a way that is not normal. These cells create tumors. Cancer tumors can start in one place, or one organ, within the body and then move to other places. When cancer moves from one organ to another, it's called a metastasis. A tumor might start out so small that it often goes undetected. By the time the tumor is large enough to be seen on an x-ray, it may cause big problems in the body. How can doctors find cancer earlier to treat and remove it? The jellyfish may be just the creature to help.

## GOING **FURTHER**

**AN X-RAY MACHINE** works by sending **ELECTROMAGNETIC BEAMS OF ENERGY** through your body. This creates an image on a **SPECIALIZED METAL FILM.** X-rays are great for **LOOKING AT BONES,** which show up as **WHITE** areas on the film. Soft tissues—organs, such as the liver, stomach, and intestines—show up as **GRAY** areas. **ON A SPECIALIZED CAMERA,** tissue that has the **GFP** attached was modified to appear **RED,** making it much easier for doctors to see.

## BUILDING BIONICS

**THE GLOWING CELLS OF A JELLYFISH** may help doctors illuminate tumors. Dr. Roger Y. Tsien is a biochemist who won a Nobel Prize for tagging cancer cells. He used a bioluminescent, or glowing, marker on a single protein to cause the cell to glow in the dark. He called this the green fluorescent protein (GFP) and initially studied it on glass slides. This started other scientists thinking: What if they used GFP to help them see cancer cells inside the body?

Scientists first had to figure out a way to get GFP into the body. They did this by attaching it to a virus—a tiny organism that infects cells. Viruses replicate, meaning they can make copies of themselves. Unlike the viruses that make you come down with a cold or flu, this engineered virus does not make people sick.

Instead, the virus is programmed to find cancer cells. When scientists insert the virus-GFP combination into a human, it finds its way to cancerous tumors hidden deep within a person's body. The GFP illuminates the tumor and makes it easier to see on a specially designed camera. The experiment has been a huge success! The technology is still being tested, but it could one day help doctors know where cancers have spread, so they can help people much faster.

◄ A DOCTOR REVIEWS X-RAY FILM OF A SKULL. THE BONES ARE HIGHLIGHTED IN WHITE.

## Did You KNOW?

**JELLYFISH** use their ability to glow to startle predators and protect themselves. Some will even drop a few of their glowing tentacles to distract a predator as the jellyfish swims away in the other direction.

## HELPFUL ADDITIONS

Scientists are excited about the possibility of using GFP to track other diseases. They could learn a lot by watching how diseases spread through the body. And one day, this could eventually help them learn enough to be able to cure or even prevent these illnesses.

# CONCLUSION

## BIONICS IN YOUR BACKYARD

**SO, WHAT DO YOU THINK** about all of these awesome, helpful, and even lifesaving inventions? Pretty incredible, huh? Animals have inspired ways to help humans walk up walls, heal wounds, vanish in plain sight, protect the environment, and do a lot of other impressive things. While many of these inventions aren't available yet, scientists and engineers are working hard to make them a reality. Every day they conduct research, build new models, test them, adjust, and then test them again. They repeat this process over and over until they come up with just the right product. So remember, all of the great inventions in this book started with observing an animal. One day, you may get an idea from watching your pet fish or a dog running around at the local park. Science is waiting for you. All you have to do is to think, imagine, and engineer it!

# GLOSSARY

▶**ACTUATOR:** a type of motor that pushes, pulls, or rotates

▶**AQUACULTURE:** raising aquatic animals or aquatic plants for food

▶**BIOLUMINESCENCE:** light given off internally by animals or organisms

▶**CAMOUFLAGE:** hiding in plain sight by means of a disguise

▶**DRAFTING:** to stay close behind another object to reduce the drag (friction)

▶**DRAG:** a force that slows an object by acting in an opposite direction to its movement

▶**HYDROPHILIC:** an object that is drawn to water

▶**HYDROPHOBIC:** an object that repels water

▶**INCANDESCENT:** light produced by incandescence (glowing radiation of heat)

▶**LED (LIGHT-EMITTING DIODE):** an electronic device that gives off light when an electrical current is passed through it

▶**MOTOR:** a machine powered by electricity or an internal combustion engine

▶**PARASITE:** an organism that lives in or on another organism

▶**pH:** the measure of the amount of hydrogen ions in a concentration

▶**PHOTOVOLTAIC:** a cell that converts light energy into electrical energy

▶**PROSTHESIS:** an artificial part of a body, like a limb

▶**ROTOR:** rotating part of a turbine

▶**SILICON:** a naturally occurring element that is used in computer chips and other machine part

▶**SILICONE:** a class of synthetic materials made up of polymers

▶**TUBERCLES:** a small, rounded ridge or outgrowth on the leading edge of a fin

# FIND OUT MORE

## BOOKS

**BIOMIMICRY: INVENTIONS INSPIRED BY NATURE** BY DORA LEE
(KIDS CAN PRESS, 2011)

**FROM CATS' EYES TO … REFLECTORS (FROM THE SERIES 21ST CENTURY SKILLS INNOVATION LIBRARY: INNOVATIONS FROM NATURE)** BY WIL MARA (CHERRY LAKE PUBLISHING, 2014)

**LAMPREYS TO ROBOTS (FROM THE SERIES 21ST CENTURY JUNIOR LIBRARY: TECH FROM NATURE)** BY JENNIFER COLBY (CHERRY LAKE PUBLISHING, 2019)

**NATURE GOT THERE FIRST: INVENTIONS INSPIRED BY NATURE** BY PHIL GATES (KINGFISHER, 2010)

**NATURE'S ENERGY (NATURE-INSPIRED INNOVATIONS)** BY ROBIN KOONTZ (ROURKE EDUCATIONAL, 2018)

**ZOOBOTS: WILD ROBOTS INSPIRED BY REAL ANIMALS** BY HELAINE BECKER (KIDS CAN PRESS, 2014)

## WEBSITES
ASK A PARENT FOR PERMISSION TO CHECK OUT THESE WEBSITES.

**THE BIOMIMICRY INSTITUTE**
BIOMIMICRY.ORG

**HOW BIOMIMICRY WORKS**
SCIENCE.HOWSTUFFWORKS.COM/LIFE/EVOLUTION/BIOMIMICRY.HTM

**LIBRARY OF CONGRESS**
HTTPS//:WWW.LOC.GOV/RR/SCITECH/MYSTERIES/BIOMIMICRY.HTML

**POPULAR SCIENCE**
HTTPS//:WWW.POPSCI.COM/TAGS/BIOMIMICRY

**WIRED: BIOMIMICRY**
HTTPS//:WWW.WIRED.COM/TAG/BIOMIMICRY

# PHOTO CREDITS

# INDEX

▶ FOR ALL YOUNG GIRLS WHO CREATE SCIENCE CLUBS IN THEIR GARAGES AND DREAM OF ONE DAY BECOMING AN ENGINEER.

Since 1888, the National Geographic Society has funded more than 12,000 research, exploration, and preservation projects around the world. The Society receives funds from National Geographic Partners, LLC, funded in part by your purchase. A portion of the proceeds from this book supports this vital work. To learn more, visit natgeo.com/info.

NATIONAL GEOGRAPHIC and Yellow Border Design are trademarks of the National Geographic Society, used under license.

For more information, visit nationalgeographic.com, call 1-877-873-6846, or write to the following address:

National Geographic Partners
1145 17th Street N.W.
Washington, DC 20036-4688 U.S.A.

Visit us online at nationalgeographic.com/books

For librarians and teachers: nationalgeographic.com/books/librarians-and-educators

More for kids from National Geographic: natgeokids.com

*National Geographic Kids* magazine inspires children to explore their world with fun yet educational articles on animals, science, nature, and more. Using fresh storytelling and amazing photography, *Nat Geo Kids* shows kids ages 6 to 14 the fascinating truth about the world—and why they should care. **kids.nationalgeographic.com/subscribe**

For rights or permissions inquiries, please contact National Geographic Books Subsidiary Rights: bookrights@natgeo.com

Library of Congress Cataloging-in-Publication Data

Names: Swanson, Jennifer, author.
Title: Beastly bionics : rad robots, brilliant biomimicry, and incredible inventions inspired by nature/Jennifer Swanson.
Description: Washington D.C. : National Geographic, 2020. | Includes bibliographical references and index. | Audience: Ages 7-10. | Audience: Grades 2-3.
Identifiers: LCCN 2019034675 | ISBN 9781426336737 (paperback) | ISBN 9781426336744 (library binding)
Subjects: LCSH: Bionics--Juvenile literature. | Biomimicry--Juvenile literature.
Classification: LCC TA164.2 .S935 2020 | DDC 629.8/92--dc23
LC record available at https://lccn.loc.gov/2019034675

Designed by Brett Challos

The publisher and author would like to thank the following people for making this book possible: Michaela Weglinski, assistant editor; Shelby Lees, senior editor; Brett Challos, art director; Shannon Hibberd, senior photo editor; Nicole DiMella, photo editor; Robin Terry-Brown, text editor; Michelle Harris, fact-checker; Robert Wood, founder of the Harvard Microrobotics Lab, and Duncan J. Irschick, professor of biology at the University of Massachusetts Amherst and director of the Digital Life Project, subject experts; and Anne LeongSon and Gus Tello, design production assistants.

Printed in Malaysia
20/QRM/1

▶ **PAGE 1:** BAT BOT DEVELOPED BY PROFESSOR SOON-JO CHUNG AND HIS TEAM AT THE UNIVERSITY OF ILLINOIS AT CHAMPAIGN–URBANA.

▶ **PAGE 2:** AN ELEPHANT GETS A "HELPING TRUNK" FROM ITS BIONIC HANDLING ASSISTANT, WHICH JUST HAPPENS TO LOOK VERY SIMILAR.